Artzeinu
AN ISRAEL ENCOUNTER

**Joel Lurie Grishaver
and Josh Mason-Barkin
with Ethan Bair**

Torah Aura Productions

Illustrations © 2008 Avi Katz.

Maps © 2008 Joe LeMonnier

All photograhs by Rabbi Chuck Briskin and Josh Mason-Barkin unless noted below.

Photo credits: Amihays, page 32; Arkady, page 112; Ayazad, page 45; Dror Bar-Natan, page 64; Iyal Bartov, page 99; Beit Hatefutsot, page 16; Erez Ben Simon, page 10; Vitaliy Berkovych, page 114; Bettmann/Corbis, pages 6, 70, 117; Alexander Biznover, pages 114; Aron Brand, pages 65, 77 ; Corky Buczyk, page 55; Joseph Calev, pages 24, 34; Ken Carey/Corbis, page 128; Gil Cohen/Reuters/Corbis, page 46; Tivadar Domaniczky, page 97; listair Duncan, page 41; Ella, pages 80, 84; Tal Engelstein and Tal Paz-Fridman, page 98; Firestone, Bryan, page 7; Gersberg, Yuri, page 63; Gileski, Dejan, page 23, 89; Hulton-Deutsch Collection/CORBIS, page 117; Hanan Isachar, page 97; Israel Ministry of Tourism, pages 39, 43, 59, 96, 99, 100, 136, 139, 141, 142, 143, 144; Kibbutz Lavi, page 101; Igor Kisselev, page 45; Wolfgang Kumm/dpa/Corbis, page 53; Mary Lane, page 105; Mikhail Levit, pages 82, 85, ; Vladislav Lopatinsky, page 116; Michael Major, page 121; Arkady Mazor, page 16; Mordechai Meiri, pages 52, 118; Eli Mordechai, pages 16, 93; Jonathan Nackstrand, page 109; Neo, page 22; Okhitin, Nikolay, page 36 ; Photos of Israel, pages 65, 66, 82; Andy Piatt, page 130; Pictorial Library of Bible Lands, pages 1, 21, 51, 58, 69, 73, 74, 79, 86, 87, 88,, 91, 107, 119 and the cover; Nola Rin, pages 75, 92; Ron Sachs/CNP/Corbis, page 111; Salamanderman, pages 28, 29, 67, 72; Oleg Seleznev, page 116; Elisei Shafer, page 115; Ted Spiegel/Corbis, page 33; Josef F. Stuefer, page 108; John Theodor/Photozion, pages 8 (top), 63 ; Dr. John C. Trever, Ph.D./Corbis, page 26; UPI/Bettmann, page 66; Hano Uzeirbegovic, 16; David V., page 115; Noam Wind, page 19; Kobi Wolf/Israel/Hadari/ZUMA/Corbis, page 56; Yuri Yavnik, page 70; Eldad Yitzhak, pages 15 (bottom), 40; Oleg Z, page 103;

Thank you to Debi Rowe and Rachel Margolis for their feedback, corrections and additions to this book.

Thank you to Susan Haubenstock and Irv Siegelman for proofing the text.

ISBN 10: 1-934527-11-4
ISBN 13: 978-1-934527-11-5

Torah Aura Productions · 4423 Fruitland Avenue, Los Angeles, CA 90058
(800) BE-Torah · (800) 238-6724 · (323) 585-7312 · fax (323) 585-0327
E-MAIL ‹misrad@torahaura.com› · Visit the Torah Aura website at www.torahaura.com
Manufactured in China   Third Printing

Table of Contents

Artzeinu

אַרְצֵנוּ

Israel is אַרְצֵנוּ *Artzeinu*. *Artzeinu* means "our land."

Israel was Jacob's other name. The Family of Israel became the Nation of Israel. The Nation of Israel moved into the Land of Canaan and made it the Land of Israel.

Jews have always lived in Israel since the return from the Babylonian Exile. There weren't always a lot of Jews, but Jews have always lived there. Israel has been ruled by the Greeks, the Romans, the Muslims, the Crusaders, the Turks, the British—and that is only the short list.

Starting in the 1800s Jews began moving back to Israel with the hope of creating a new Jewish State. חֲלוּצִים *Halutzim* (pioneers) moved to Israel, bought land, and settled it. In some cases they turned swamps into fertile fields. A lot of things happened: World War I, World War II, the Holocaust, and a United Nations resolution.

In 1948 the new State of Israel was born. Israel was reborn. Jews from all around the world began the process of making Israel a modern, democratic, creative, inventive force. Israel, a Hebrew-speaking nation that struggles with how religious and non-religious live together, with how Jew and non–Jew share a Jewish state, that has lots of problems and lots of opportunities, has become the Jewish homeland.

Israel is the place where any Jew from around the world can find safety and freedom. It is a place that works daily on creating and growing Jewish culture. It is *Artzeinu*, our Land.

Faces Of Israel—Moriah (http://tiny.cc/k7por)

Meet Israel

Israel is about the size of New Jersey (even if its shape is much narrower). It is surrounded by the Arab states of Lebanon, Syria, Jordan, and Egypt. It is now at peace with half of them. It also contains (at the moment) the West Bank and it surrounds most of Gaza. The country has mountains and beaches, desert and green forests. It is always growing and changing.

Label the following places on the map.

Tel Aviv is a combination of the New York and the Miami of Israel. It is a big modern city built on the shores of the Mediterranean Sea. It is a center of business and a great place to play, too.

The Dead Sea is between Israel and Jordan at the end of the River Jordan. It is the lowest place in the world and has a very high mineral content. You can't sink in the Dead Sea. It is a place of recreation and a place where a lot of archeology is done.

Haifa is a major port city. It is to the North of Tel Aviv on the Mediterranean Sea. Haifa is built on the side of a mountain like San Francisco. When you look at the city the first thing you see is the Golden Dome of the Baha'i Shrine.

Jerusalem is two cities in one. There is the ancient "Old City" that goes back before the time of King David and there is the new, modern city, that is the capital of Israel. On one hand there is the Dome of the Rock, an ancient Muslim site with a golden Dome and on the other there is the *K'nesset*, the parliament of Israel.

The Galilee is in the North of Israel. It is a series of valleys and mountains and a big lake, the *Kineret*. It is a place of kibbutzin, villages, small cities and towns. Next to the Galilee are the high mountains of the Golan that has Israel's only ski resort.

Negev means "dry." The Negev is the southern part of Israel. It is mainly desert but it includes the city of Beersheva and the beach city of Eilat. Ben Gurion chose to spend the end of his life in the Negev because it is the frontier of Israel.

Tzfat is a city in the North of Israel. It is an artists' colony and a place of Jewish mystical study. Mystics lived there. Mystics still learn and teach there. It is in Tzfat that the custom of going out to the fields to welcome Shabbat began.

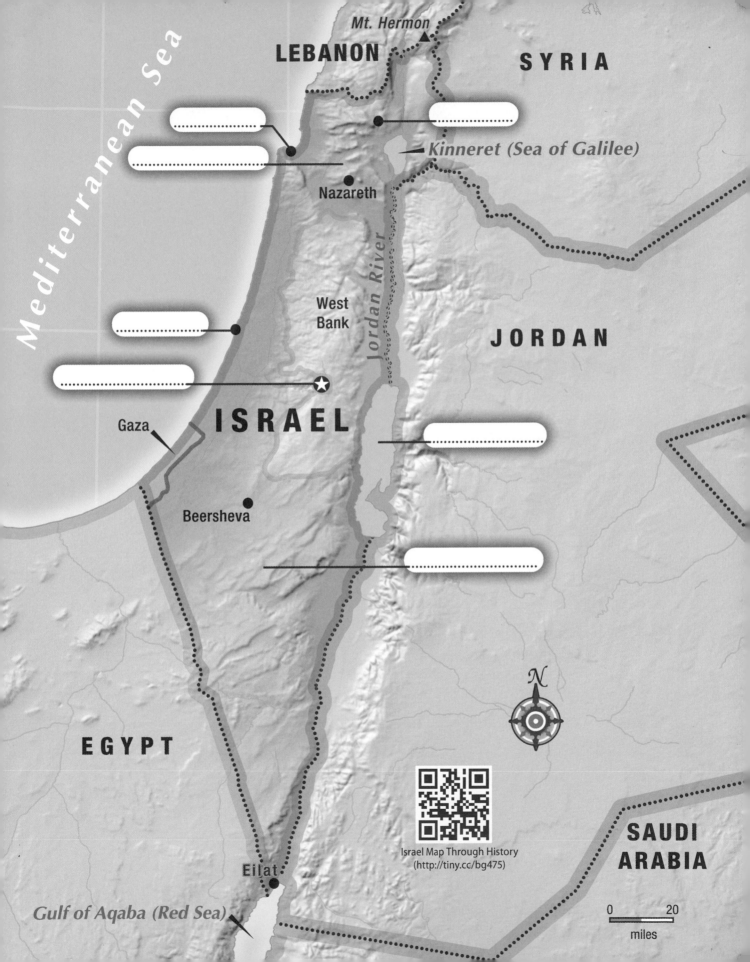

Mt. Hermon

LEBANON

SYRIA

Mediterranean Sea

Kinneret (Sea of Galilee)

Nazareth

Jordan River

West
Bank

JORDAN

ISRAEL

Gaza

Beersheva

N

EGYPT

Israel Map Through History
(http://tiny.cc/bg475)

SAUDI
ARABIA

Eilat

Gulf of Aqaba (Red Sea)

0   20

miles

Tel Aviv

תֵּל אָבִיב

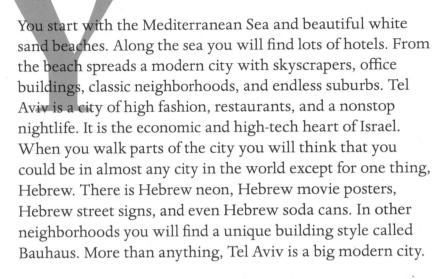

You start with the Mediterranean Sea and beautiful white sand beaches. Along the sea you will find lots of hotels. From the beach spreads a modern city with skyscrapers, office buildings, classic neighborhoods, and endless suburbs. Tel Aviv is a city of high fashion, restaurants, and a nonstop nightlife. It is the economic and high-tech heart of Israel. When you walk parts of the city you will think that you could be in almost any city in the world except for one thing, Hebrew. There is Hebrew neon, Hebrew movie posters, Hebrew street signs, and even Hebrew soda cans. In other neighborhoods you will find a unique building style called Bauhaus. More than anything, Tel Aviv is a big modern city.

The History of Tel Aviv

The history of Tel Aviv teaches us a lot about the history of Israel.

Tel Aviv has its origins in an ancient city called Jaffa (*Yafo*). Jaffa goes back to the Bible. It was given to the Tribe of Dan, used as a port for the cedars used in Solomon's Temple, and was the place from which Jonah fled from God. During the time of the Crusades it was the Country of Yafo that was a stronghold of the Kingdom of Jerusalem.

In 1909 a group of sixty Jewish families who were living in Jaffa decided that a crowded and expensive city was not their idea of the "Zionist Dream." Zionism was the movement that brought Jews back to the Land of Israel, that dreamed of creating a Jewish State. They bought some property north of Jaffa and set up a settlement creatively called *Ahuzat Bayit* (housing property). A year later Mena<u>h</u>em Sheinkin, an activist in the <u>*Hovevei Zion*</u> (Lovers of Zion) organization, suggested to the local council that they change the name to Tel Aviv. He was one of the founders of *Herzliya Gymnasium*, the first Hebrew high school in Israel.

Tel Aviv—Life and Street Culture (http://tiny.cc/gg4fj)

In 1909, members of two Zionist groups gathered in the desert near Jaffa in Turkish-ruled Palestine to cast lots for building sites. These Jews worked and lived in Jaffa, a 3,500 year-old Arab city, but decided to build the first all-Jewish city in 2,000 years. They named it Tel Aviv, literally "Hill of Spring."

The Name "Tel Aviv"

Of course, the name "Tel Aviv" has a story. In the book of Ezekiel (3.15) a place called תֵּל אָבִיב Tel Aviv is mentioned. No one to this day has any idea where that Tel Aviv is. We do know that Tel Aviv sort of means "Hill of Spring." But a תֵּל Tel is not an ordinary hill, but rather a hill built up of a series of cities that were built over the ruins of previous cities.

Theodor Herzl was the founder of modern Zionism. In 1902 he wrote a novel called *Altneuland,* which translates literally as "Old New Land." It was about the creation of an idealistic, wonderful future for the Jewish people. The book's motto was:

If you will it, it is no fairy-tale. But if you do not will it, it is and will remain a fairy-tale, this story that I have told you…All the activity of humankind was a dream once…

Tel Aviv is the title given by Nahum Sokolow to his 1902 translation of Theodor Herzl's book, with *Tel* being the old state that was destroyed and *Aviv* being the new spring a new State could bring.

The Shell Lottery

People who live in Tel Aviv tell the story of the "Shell Lottery". To make sure the distribution of the land was fair, Arieh Akiva Weiss, the original community leader, collected sixty white shells on which he wrote the names of the families and sixty

6

gray shells on which he wrote the numbers of the plots. The pairs of gray and white shells determined which family got which plot of land. This story says that a city by the sea was created using shells off its beach.

Sheinkin Street

Remember Menahem Sheinkin? He was the one who suggested that the new city be named Tel Aviv. Today in modern Tel Aviv there is a Sheinkin Street. It is one of the busiest and hippest places in Israel. It is a street with its own web page, (www.sheinkinstreet.co.il), and it is Tel Aviv's Friday morning hot spot. Whether it's summer or winter, early in the morning or late at night, Sheinkin does not sleep.

Early photographs show Sheinkin Street with rectangular houses and green-topped trees. It was a quiet place and the continuation of the special building design of Rothschild Boulevard and Allenby Street that surrounds Sheinkin from both sides. The *Davar* newspaper building stood on the corner of Sheinkin and Melkhet Street. The writers of the newspaper spent much of their time drinking coffee in nearby Café Tamar, a place that still exists. Over the years Sheinkin became a street filled with out-of-date shops, and the only people who lived there were older immigrants from Europe that settled in the cheapest stretch of real estate that was close to the beach. Sheinkin was just another street, a place you crossed on your way to the busy Allenby Street.

Meir Dizengoff

Dizengoff Square

Meir Dizengoff (1861–1936) was the first mayor of Tel Aviv. He wanted to create a city that would at once be cosmopolitan, culturally alive, and entirely new.

One day he invited the media to the opening of the new Tel Aviv port. Everyone who came saw only sand, blue water, and sky. He pounded a stick into the sand for a "ground-breaking," and now all that was visible was sand, blue water, sky, and a stick in the ground. He then announced to the crowd, "Ladies and gentlemen, I still remember the day when Tel Aviv had no port."

The main street in Tel Aviv is named after him—Dizengoff Street—and it boasts many cultural centers, cafés, shopping, and galleries. There is even a verb named after Dizengoff. In Hebrew slang, לְהִזְדַּנְגֵּף *l'hizdangef* means "to go out on the town," to stroll the streets of downtown enjoyably.

1. What about Dizengoff's personality made him a perfect first mayor of Tel Aviv?

2. Where in Israel would you like to *hizdangef*?

Shlomo "Chich" Lahat, former mayor of Tel Aviv (in the years 1973–1993), was the one to understand the real potential of Sheinkin. He was the one who started Sheinkin's revival. Artists, writers, and musicians who were attracted to the new vibe and the many coffee shops came to live on the street. The two Dotan brothers came to realize that Sheinkin needed a new cultural center, so they opened the Café/Gallery. This artist center made the street distinctive.

The journalist and television presenter Yair Lapid spoke of this in his lyrics for the song *Gara Be-Sheinkin* ("Living in Sheinkin"), sung by the girl band Mango. This song celebrated the cliché image of the original Sheinkin woman dressed all in black, drinking coffee in Café Tamar and dreaming of being in the movies.

Street Names

Israeli street names, for the most part, are history lessons. Israeli streets are named after famous people (not all Jews), all of whom had some big influence on Israel. For instance, both Tel Aviv and Jerusalem have a Lincoln Street because of the value of personal freedom he modeled.

Here are four potential street names and mini-biographies. Check the one that you would choose for a new street in a new Israeli city. (F.Y.I.: All these are already streets in the Sheinkin area of Tel Aviv).

____ Balfour

Arthur James Balfour (1848–1930) was the prime minister of Britain. The name Balfour became known as result of the historic Balfour Declaration that he authored in 1917. It promised the Jews a national home in Israel.

____ Melchett

Lord Alfred Melchett first visited Palestine in 1921 with Chaim Weitzmann, then president of the World Zionist Organization, and began contributing money to the Jewish Colonization Corporation for Palestine and writing for Zionist publications.

____ Mazeh

Rabbi Ya'akov Mazeh was the chief rabbi of Moscow and a member of *Hovevei Zion* (Friends of Zion) society. He became famous as a key witness in the Beilis trial. He proved false the blood libel accusations (Jews killing Christians for ritual purposes), and as an expert in the Torah.

____ Ahad Ha'am

Ahad Ha'am (1856–1927) was born Asher Zvi Ginsburg. He was one of the leaders of *Hovevei Zion*. In 1889 he wrote an article about the need of the Jewish people for their own homeland, entitled "This Is Not the Way." He signed this article Ahad Ha'am, which in English means "One of the People." Ahad Ha'am Street is where Ahad Ha'am used to live.

After whom would you name an Israeli street?

_____

_____

_____

Gal Abulafia

My name is Gal Abulafia. My family comes from Morocco. I share the name Gal with Gal Mekel, a great basketball player and Gal Friedman who won an Olympic gold metal for windsurfing. I share the name Abulafia with Abraham ben Samuel Abulafia, a famous Kabbalistic rabbi from the 13th century. My family came to Israel from Casablanca in the mid-nineteen-fifties.

One of the great dishes my mother makes is *Dafina*. It is a traditional Shabbat meal made of wheat, dried peas and meat this is slowly cooked overnight in a low-temp oven. The word comes from Arabic "*dafina* or *adafina*" meaning "covered" or "smothered".

My favorite sport is "*Kadur Sal*," basketball. I am not that tall, but I have a good layup and a good outside jump shot. My favorite team is Maccabi Tel-Aviv.

We Moroccan Jews have our own holiday called the *Mamoona*. It is named after Maimonides and it takes place on the night or the day after Passover. My mother makes all kinds of pastries that we couldn't eat the previous week. Some Moroccan families have a party on the night after Passover. My family gets together with other Moroccan families and has a big picnic and cookout on that day.

Tel Aviv–Yafo

There is Tel Aviv–Yafo and there is greater Tel Aviv. In 1950, because they had basically grown into each other, Tel Aviv-Yafo merged into a single city. Today about 390,000 people live there. Greater Tel Aviv includes Holon (170,000), Petah Tikvah (200,000), Bat Yam (150,000), Bene Barak (150,000), Ramat Gan (140,000), etc. When you add in all of the small cities and independent suburbs that are part of greater Tel Aviv, the number grows to 3.1 million people.

Besides attracting tourism, Tel Aviv is a major commercial and financial center. It also has a lot of manufacturing and industry. At the same time it is a cultural center with two major universities (Tel Aviv University and Bar Ilan) and the headquarters of Habima (the national theatre) and the Israel Philharmonic Orchestra. Many newspapers and magazines have their editorial offices in Tel Aviv. Not bad for a housing development set up by sixty families about a hundred years ago.

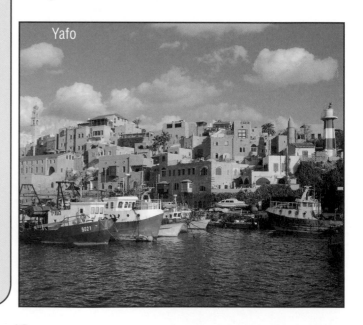
Yafo

Independence Hall

To understand modern Israel we need to understand another piece of early Tel Aviv history. Today you can visit a large home on Rothschild Boulevard that is known as Independence Hall. It is here that Israel's Declaration of Independence was signed. Today it is a museum, but in 1909 it was where Meir Dizengoff drew plot forty-three in the original *Ahuzat Bayit* lottery, and it was where a year later the meeting was held where Mena<u>h</u>em Sheinkin suggested the new name Tel Aviv and won that vote. Meir Dizengoff became Mayor Dizengoff when he was elected Tel Aviv's mayor. The house became the mayor's office.

In 1939, after Dizengoff's death, his wife Zina donated the house to the city of Tel Aviv, and it became the Tel Aviv Art Museum. On May 14, 1948, David Ben-Gurion, Israel's first Prime Minister, proclaimed the establishment of the State of Israel in the main hall of the building. After Ben-Gurion read the declaration of independence, Rabbi Fishman recited the *She-he-<u>h</u>eyanu* blessing, and the Declaration of Independence was signed. The ceremony concluded with the singing of *Ha-Tikvah*, the Israeli national anthem.

In 1978 Independence Hall was restored and opened to the public. It is now a museum that deals with the signing of the Declaration of Independence and the history of Tel Aviv–Yafo.

11

THE DECLARATION OF THE ESTABLISHMENT OF THE STATE OF ISRAEL, May 14, 1948

1

a. What is "the eternal Book of Books?"

b. Does this reference make the writers of this document religious?

c. What history are they talking about in this paragraph?

2–3

d. What story is being told in these two paragraphs?

e. Who are "the pioneers" being mentioned?

4–5

f. Why is Theodor Herzl the only person mentioned by name in this document?

g. What was the Balfour Declaration?

h. What was the League of Nations?

6–7

i. How is the Holocaust used to justify the creation of a State of Israel?

j. What is meant by "undaunted by difficulties, restrictions and dangers, and never ceased to assert their right to a life of dignity, freedom and honest toil in their national homeland"?

[1]ERETZ-ISRAEL was the birthplace of the Jewish people. Here their spiritual, religious and political identity was shaped. Here they first attained statehood, created cultural values of national and universal significance, and gave to the world the eternal Book of Books.

[2]After being forcibly exiled from their land, the people kept faith with it throughout their Dispersion and never ceased to pray and hope for their return to it and for the restoration in it of their political freedom.

[3]Impelled by this historic and traditional attachment, Jews strove in every successive generation to re-establish themselves in their ancient homeland. In recent decades they returned in their masses. Pioneers and defenders, they made deserts bloom, revived the Hebrew language, built villages and towns, and created a thriving community controlling its own economy and culture, loving peace but knowing how to defend itself, bringing the blessings of progress to all the country's inhabitants, and aspiring towards independent nationhood.

[4]In the year 5657 (1897), at the summons of the spiritual father of the Jewish State, Theodor Herzl, the First Zionist Congress convened and proclaimed the right of the Jewish people to national rebirth in its own country.

[5]This right was recognized in the Balfour Declaration of the 2nd November, 1917, and re-affirmed in the Mandate of the League of Nations which, in particular, gave international sanction to the historic connection between the Jewish people and Eretz-Israel and to the right of the Jewish people to rebuild its National Home.

[6]The catastrophe which recently befell the Jewish people—the massacre of millions of Jews in Europe—was another clear demonstration of the urgency of solving the problem of its homelessness by re-establishing in Eretz-Israel the Jewish State, which would open the gates of the homeland wide to every Jew and confer upon the Jewish people the status of a fully privileged member of the comity of nations.

[7]Survivors of the Nazi holocaust in Europe, as well as Jews from other parts of the world, continued to migrate to Eretz-Israel, undaunted by difficulties, restrictions and dangers, and never ceased to assert their right to a life of dignity, freedom and honest toil in their national homeland.

[8]In the Second World War, the Jewish community of this country contributed its full share to the struggle of the freedom- and peace-loving nations against the forces of Nazi wickedness and, by the blood of its soldiers and its war effort, gained the right to be reckoned among the peoples who founded the United Nations.

[9]On the 29th November, 1947, the United Nations General Assembly passed a resolution calling for the establishment of a Jewish State in Eretz-Israel; the General Assembly required the inhabitants of Eretz-Israel to take such steps as were necessary on their part for the implementation of that resolution. This recognition by the United Nations of the right of the Jewish people to establish their State is irrevocable.

[10]This right is the natural right of the Jewish people to be masters of their own fate, like all other nations, in their own sovereign State.

[11]ACCORDINGLY WE, MEMBERS OF THE PEOPLE'S COUNCIL, representatives of the Jewish community of Eretz-Israel and of the Zionist movement, are here assembled on the day of the termination of the British Mandate over Eretz-Israel and, by virtue of our natural and historic right and on the strength of the resolution of the United Nations general assembly, hereby declare the establishment of a Jewish State in Eretz-Israel, to be known as the State of Israel.

[12]WE DECLARE that, with effect from the moment of the termination of the Mandate being tonight, the eve of Sabbath, the 6th Iyar, 5708 (15th May, 1948), until the establishment of the elected, regular authorities of the State in accordance with the Constitution which shall be adopted by the Elected Constituent Assembly not later than the 1st October 1948, the People's Council shall act as a Provisional Council of State, and its executive organ, the People's Administration, shall be the Provisional Government of the Jewish State, to be called "Israel".

[13]THE STATE OF ISRAEL will be open for Jewish immigration and for the Ingathering of the Exiles; it will foster the development of the country for the benefit of all its inhabitants; it will be based on freedom, justice and peace as envisaged by the prophets of Israel; it will ensure complete equality of social and political rights to all its inhabitants irrespective of religion, race or sex; it will guarantee freedom of religion, conscience, language, education and culture; it will safeguard the

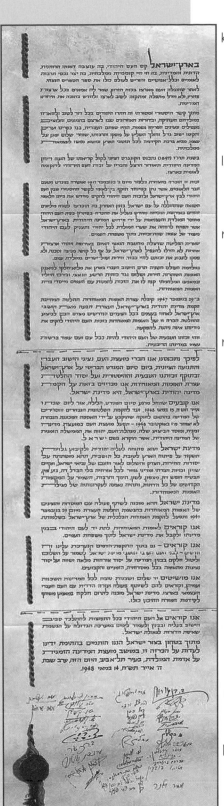

8–10

k. What is being referred to by "the Jewish community of this country contributed its full share to the struggle of the freedom- and peace-loving nations against the forces of Nazi wickedness"?

l. How does this become an argument for the establishment of the State of Israel?

m. Why did the writers add "This recognition by the United Nations of the right of the Jewish people to establish their State is irrevocable"?

n. What is a "natural right"?

Declaration of Independence of the State of Israel (http://tiny.cc/7p1n1)

13

o. What vision of the future state is found in paragraph 13?

p. What is meant by "ingathering of the exiles"?

14–16

q. What is the hope of these four paragraphs?

r. How well has this happened?

17–19

s. What is "the Diaspora"?

t. What is being asked of the world Jewish community?

u. What is "the rock of Israel"? Why do you think this term is used?

v. Is this a religious document?

Holy Places of all religions; and it will be faithful to the principles of the Charter of the United Nations.

[14]THE STATE OF ISRAEL is prepared to cooperate with the agencies and representatives of the United Nations in implementing the resolution of the General Assembly of the 29th November, 1947, and will take steps to bring about the economic union of the whole of Eretz-Israel.

[15]WE APPEAL to the United Nations to assist the Jewish people in the building-up of its State and to receive the State of Israel into the comity of nations.

[16]WE APPEAL—in the very midst of the onslaught launched against us now for months—to the Arab inhabitants of the State of Israel to preserve peace and participate in the upbuilding of the State on the basis of full and equal citizenship and due representation in all its provisional and permanent institutions.

[17]WE EXTEND our hand to all neighboring states and their peoples in an offer of peace and good neighborliness, and appeal to them to establish bonds of cooperation and mutual help with the sovereign Jewish people settled in its own land. The State of Israel is prepared to do its share in a common effort for the advancement of the entire Middle East.

[18]WE APPEAL to the Jewish people throughout the Diaspora to rally round the Jews of Eretz-Israel in the tasks of immigration and upbuilding and to stand by them in the great struggle for the realization of the age-old dream—the redemption of Israel.

[19]PLACING OUR TRUST IN THE "ROCK OF ISRAEL", we affix our signatures to this proclamation at this session of the provisional council of State, on the soil of the homeland, in the city of Tel-Aviv, on this Sabbath eve, the 5th day of Iyar, 5708 (14th May, 1948).

David Ben-Gurion	Herzl Vardi	Moshe Shapira
Daniel Auster	David Zvi Pinkas	Moshe Shertok
Mordekhai Bentov	Aharon Zisling	Rachel Cohen
Yitzchak Ben Zvi	Moshe Kolodny	Rabbi Kalman Kahana
Eliyahu Berligne	Eliezer Kaplan	Saadia Kobashi
Fritz Bernstein	Abraham Katznelson	Rabbi Yitzchak Meir Levin
Rabbi Wolf Gold	Felix Rosenblueth	Meir David Loewenstein
Meir Grabovsky	David Remez	Zvi Luria
Yitzchak Gruenbaum	Berl Repetur	Golda Myerson
Dr. Abraham Granovsky	Mordekhai Shattner	Nachum Nir
Eliyahu Dobkin	Ben Zion Sternberg	Zvi Segal
Meir Wilner-Kovner	Bekhor Shitreet	Rabbi Yehuda Leib Hacohen Fishman
Zerach Wahrhaftig		

• Published in the Official Gazette, No. 1 of the 5th Iyar, 5708 (14th May, 1948).

Five "Don't Miss" Places in Tel Aviv-Yafo

The Palmakh Museum is probably Israel's coolest museum experience. It tells the story of the Palmakh. The Palmakh was the elite striking force of the Haganah—the underground military organization of the Jewish community before the founding of the State of Israel. During the War of Independence they operated all over the country, liberating Jerusalem and other besieged towns, and with the newly organized Haganah troops they defeated the invading armies of Egypt, Syria, Jordan, Lebanon, and Iraq.

The museum unfolds through the stories of individuals and groups. There are no displays or documents; rather, the museum uses three-dimensional decor, films, and various effects. Visitors to the museum join a group of young Palmakh recruits from its establishment and move through the story of the Palmakh until the end of the War of Independence.

The Herbert Samuel Promenade (named after the first British governor-general under the Mandate) is known as the טַיֶלֶת *Tayelet*. In Hebrew לְטַיֵּל *L'Tayel* means "to stroll." The *Tayelet* offers great people-watching. You'll see the beautiful people with their unbelievably fit bodies and elderly Russian ladies strolling arm in arm. You'll see Jewish and Arab families out for a swim. All along you'll hear the sound of the surf and smell the salt air. When you get down to Yafo the view back to Tel Aviv is stunning.

The White City

The White City is Tel Aviv's nickname because of the number of white or light-colored buildings built there between the 1920s and the 1950s in the Bauhaus style. Over 4,000 buildings in this style can still be seen in central Tel Aviv.

Jews from Germany began to arrive after the election of the Nazis to power in 1933. Some of them were builders, craftsmen, and architects who were trained and influenced by the Bauhaus architectural school.

The Bauhaus style was created to reflect the union of art and functional use in post–World War I Europe. In Tel Aviv the style seemed ideal. Buildings could be erected quickly and cheaply.

Bauhaus is characterized by many horizontal lines—like windows and flat roofs—maximizing space inside the structure. In Israel, because of the heat, balconies almost always replaced mere windows.

Bauhaus Tel Aviv Exhibit at Brandeis University (http://tiny.cc/nb7r0)

The *Tayelet* is three and a half miles long, 15 to 25 feet wide and is paved with patterned and swirled stone. The *Tayelet*'s walkway, shaded pergolas, chairs, palm trees, and flower beds have transformed Tel Aviv's once-drab seafront into an Eastern Mediterranean version of Nice or Rio de Janeiro. Every few blocks the *Tayelet* sprouts an outdoor restaurant or a café, and it is crowded day and night with strollers, dog-walkers, joggers, entertainers, Rollerbladers, craftspeople, and, of course, Tel Avivians and tourists.

Rabin Square is a large public square in central Tel Aviv. It is named after Israeli Prime Minister Yitzhak Rabin, who was assassinated there in 1995. Rabin Square is the largest open public square in Tel Aviv and is known for holding many political rallies, parades, and other public events. On the days following the assassination thousands of Israelis gathered on the site to commemorate Rabin. The young people who came to mourn Rabin were dubbed the "Candles Youth" after the many yahrzeit candles they lit. Some of the graffiti they drew upon the nearby walls remains. Today a memorial can be found on the site where Rabin was assassinated.

Yafo

Old Yafo. According to Christian legend, Yafo was named after Noah's son Japhet, who built it after the Flood. There are others who believe that the name derives from the Hebrew word *yofi*—beauty. Old Yafo is filled with artists' quarters, studios, and art galleries. Shops catering to buyers of Judaica, archaeology, and jewelry line its narrow alleys, which are named after the signs of the Zodiac. Visitors from both Israel and abroad enjoy dining in its unique restaurants or simply wandering around.

Beit Hatefutsot is "The Diaspora House"—the Nahum Goldmann Museum of the Jewish Diaspora, established in 1978. It is located at Tel Aviv University. When it opened it was regarded by many museum experts as one of the most innovative museums in the world. The museum uses modern techniques and audiovisual displays to trace the history of the communities of the Jewish diaspora through the ages and around the world and to tell the story of the Jewish people from the time of their exile from the Land of Israel 2,500 years ago to the present.

CHALLENGE FOR ISRAEL POVERTY

Israel has a large discrepancy between rich and poor that is second only to the United States. That means that although it is a relatively rich country, a huge part of the population does not feel it. A quarter of Israeli children are living in poverty. Fully one half of Arab Israeli children live below the poverty line. (For comparison, the child poverty figure is only 3% for Scandinavian countries.) This percentage is embarrassingly high.

Many Haredi (ultra–Orthodox) families live below the poverty line because of the combination of unemployment and high birth rates found among them, often as a choice (even though the government pays subsidies for having many children). Also, Arab Israelis suffer the highest unemployment and poverty rates within Israel.

They are segments of the population that do not serve in the IDF. It is very hard in Israel to get a good job without having served in the military. This fact indirectly puts non–Jews and the ultra–Orthodox in Israel at a disadvantage in finding good jobs.

When Israel was founded, the government set up many programs to help new immigrants and people who were poor. In recent decades, the government has been under pressure to lower taxes. As a result, there has been less money to pay for these programs, and poverty is now a very serious problem in Israel. Just like other modern countries, Israel is balancing the divide between a population that is economically successful while some people remain in poverty.

You Be the Tour Guide

Tel Aviv is a great place to be a tourist. There are great museums, fabulous shopping, and amazing beaches. And that is only the start. You be the tour guide for a day. Plan a schedule that has something for everyone in the family.

Abba (Dad)

Loves sports, being outdoors and reading mystery novels.

Ima (Mom)

Loves shopping, swimming, theater, and sunset walks on the beach.

David (age 12)

Likes the beach, skateboarding, animals, and history.

Arielle (age 9)

Is really into music, loves sports, and good food.

Dov

Likes to eat, sleep, and chase his tail.

Activities

* Catch a football (soccer) game at Bloomfield Stadium in Yafo.
* Rent a boat at Sea Center in the Tel Aviv Marina.
* Water-ski in the artificial lake at Park Darom.
• Learn about a famous Israeli poet at Bet Bialik Museum.
• See a play at Habimah Theatre, home of Israel's national theatre company.
• Visit the museum at Independence Hall, the house where the Declaration of Independence was signed.
• Visit the gift shops at Kikar Kedumin in Yafo.
• See dazzling gems at the Harry Oppenheimer Diamond Museum.
• Stroll around and check out the fancy houses in Neve Tzedek, Tel Aviv's most stylish neighborhood.
• Catch a movie and go shopping at Dizengoff Center.
• Watch the wild animals roam free at Safari Park in Ramat Gan.
• Hear the Zion Symphony Orchestra in concert at the Tel Aviv Performing Arts Center.

Restaurants

- Chicago Pizza Pie Factory: Deep-dish or thin-crust American-style pizza.
- Mul-Yam: The freshest seafood in Israel.
- Café Cazeh: Vegetarian delights!
- Bebale: Old-style Jewish food.
- Cactus: American-style Tex-Mex.
- Keren: One of Israel's fanciest restaurants.
- Shipudei Hatikva: Family-style Israeli food.
- Tandoori: Spicy Indian curries and exotic flavors.
- Yossi's Falafel
- Ben & Jerry's Ice Cream

SCHEDULE	THINGS TO DO	RESTAURANTS
9:00 a.m. to 10:00 a.m.	Breakfast	
10:00 a.m. to 11:00 a.m.		
11:00 a.m. to 12:00 p.m.		
12:00 p.m. to 1:00 p.m.	Lunch	
1:00 p.m. to 2:00 p.m.		
2:00 p.m. to 3:00 p.m.		
3:00 p.m. to 4:00 p.m.	Afternoon snack	
4:00 p.m. to 5:00 p.m.		
5:00 p.m. to 6:00 p.m.		
6:00 p.m. to 7:00 p.m.	Dinner	

The Dead Sea

I The Geography

If you look at a satellite map of the Middle East you can see a deep valley that starts up in Turkey and heads down to the Gulf of Aqaba. This Great Rift actually heads through Africa as well. About three million years ago the valley of the Dead Sea was flooded by the Mediterranean Sea. One million years later the land between the Mediterranean and the Jordan Rift Valley rose so that the seawater stopped flooding the area. What was formed was an inland lake, the Dead Sea. Up north there is the Kinneret, the Sea of Galilee; it is a freshwater lake. From the Kinneret flows the Jordan River down into the Dead Sea, which is a mineral-laden salt sea.

The lowest point in the Jordan Rift Valley is at the shore of the Dead Sea that is also the lowest point on the surface of the earth, at 400 meters below sea level. Along the Jordan River is a lush green area. Surrounding the Dead Sea is a desert where there is almost no fresh water.

Archaeology

Almost everyone in Israel is into archaeology. Archaeology is the process of reconstructing the lives of people who lived before us from the artifacts they left behind. Archaeology is digging, documenting, preserving, and then using what you've found to put together an idea of what life was like in a given place and time. Israel is an amazing place for archaeology. No matter where you walk in Israel, history is underfoot. Israeli archaeology starts with the Neolithic Era (back to 8500 B.C.E.), goes through the Bronze Age (Abraham and company), the Iron Age (King David and friends), the Persian occupation, the Helenistic and Roman eras, the Byzantines, the Arab Caliphate, the Crusaders, the Mamluk and Ottomans, and the British Mandate and comes all the way forward to the early history of the State of Israel. That is a lot of stuff to dig up.

Dead Sea Floating...a demonstration (http://tiny.cc/k18ux)

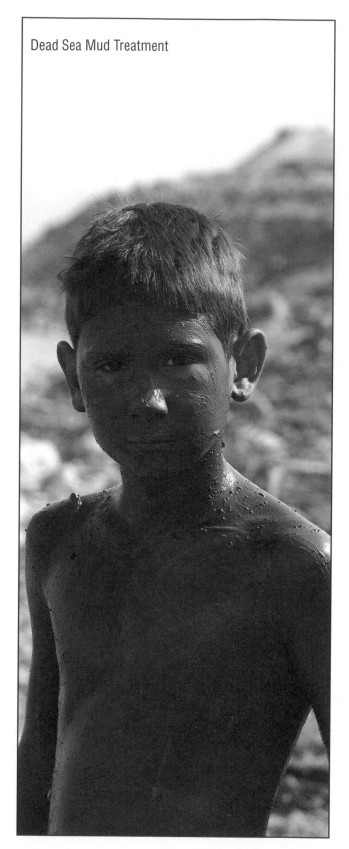

Dead Sea Mud Treatment

Jordan River

Jericho

Jerusalem

Qumran

Bethlehem

Nakhal Ovnat

Ein Gedi

Masada

ISRAEL

JORDAN

Dead Sea

N

0   10
miles

Our visit to the Dead Sea is primarily an archaeological visit. On the Israeli side of the Dead Sea (Jordan has the other side) are a few kibbutzim, some hotels, some industry, and some really important archaeological sites. We have Qumran, the source of the Dead Sea Scrolls. There is Ein Gedi, an important place in the King David story. And there is Masada, a former palace of King Herod that became the last siege of the Sicarii after the fall of Jerusalem.

One of the most chaotic periods of Jewish history was the first century C.E. (the years 1–100). Josephus, a famous Jewish Roman historian from this period, writes: "For there are three philosophical sects among the Jews. The followers of the first of which are the Pharisees; of the second, the Sadducees; and the third sect, which opts for a more severe discipline, are called Essenes" (*The Jewish Wars*, Book II, Chapter 8). Most of the history we will encounter at the Dead Sea comes from this period, which is filled with revolts, chaos, and even the creation of Christianity.

Qumran Caves

Qumran

Qumran is located on a dry plateau about a mile inland from the northwestern shore of the Dead Sea just next to the Israeli kibbutz of Kalia. It is best known as the settlement nearest to the hiding place of the Dead Sea Scrolls in the caves of the sheer desert cliffs.

In 1947 two Bedouin shepherds accidentally came across a clay jar in a cave near Khirbet Qumran that contained seven parchment scrolls. These Dead Sea scrolls came into the hands of dealers in antiquities who offered them to scholars. The first scholar to recognize their antiquity was E.L. Sukenik, who succeeded in acquiring three of them for the Hebrew University. The four other scrolls were smuggled to the United States. Later they were offered for sale in a unusual newspaper ad under the heading "Miscellaneous for Sale." Sukenik's son Yigael Yadin, also an outstanding archaeologist, succeeded in buying them and bringing them back to Israel. The Israel Museum in Jerusalem constructed a special site for exhibiting the scrolls—the Shrine of the Book.

It is generally accepted that a Bedouin goat- or sheep-herder by the name of Mohammed Ahmed el-Hamed (nicknamed *edh-Dhib*, "the wolf") made the first discovery toward the beginning of 1947. In the most commonly told story the shepherd threw a rock into a cave in an attempt to drive out a missing animal under his care. The sound of shattering pottery drew him into the cave, where he found several ancient jars containing scrolls wrapped in linen.

Qumran Ruins

24

Since 1947 nearly 900 scrolls in various states of completeness, mostly written on parchment, have been found.

Explaining Qumran

Archaeology is all about using evidence to figure out what has happened in the past. Imagine that you found a wastebasket with a hamburger wrapper (with a pickle still in it), a bottle of milk, and a ripped kippah. The question is, what can you learn about the person who threw the stuff in the wastebasket? You can come up with a number of different conclusions.

a. The wastebasket belonged to a Jew who didn't keep kosher (because the person had milk with meat).

b. The wastebasket belonged to a Jew who did keep kosher but ate the milk and the meat at different times.

c. The wastebasket belonged to a non–Jew who picked up a kippah at some Jewish event he attended as a guest.

All three of these answers are possible. The facts support more than one hypothesis. The same is true of the archaeology at Qumran.

Some people believe that the Dead Sea Scrolls are the writings of the Essenes. They were a highly-ritualistic sect who were busy waiting for the end of the world. Another theory is that these are documents smuggled out of Jerusalem before the destruction of the Temple. There are lots more theories about the scrolls, too.

Qumran—The Story Of The Dead Sea Scrolls (http://tiny.cc/lq4we)

Ruti Kaufman

My name is Ruti. In English you would say Ruthy. My family comes from Jerusalem and we are at the Dead Sea because it is cold in Jerusalem and warm down here. When it is cold and rainy in Jerusalem it is nice to come to the Dead Sea and wear a bathing suit.

I love dancing. I take ballet lessons and I go folk dancing with my youth movement. I have danced in professional ballets twice and I dance on an Israeli dance team.

My family comes from Poland. They moved to Israel back before there was a state when it was still Palestine. People think that everyone from Jerusalem is religious but my family isn't. We are _hiloni_, that is Hebrew for "secular." I love Yom Kippur because it is a day when I can ride my bicycle on the street with no worry about any cars.

My favorite food that my mother cooks is her chicken schnitzel. Schnitzel, which means cutlet in German, originally referred to deep-fried, breaded veal cutlets. The name and idea were borrowed by Jews, and today Israeli children like me are practically raised on chicken schnitzel.

The Dead Sea Scrolls

The Isaiah Scroll, found relatively intact, is 1,000 years older than any previously known copy of Isaiah. The scrolls are the oldest group of biblical manuscripts ever found. However, not all of the scrolls are biblical texts.

One of the most curious scrolls is the Copper Scroll. Discovered in Cave 3, this scroll records a list of 64 underground hiding places. The deposits in these places are to contain certain amounts of gold, silver, perfumes, and manuscripts. Some believe they are treasures from the Temple at Jerusalem that were hidden away for safekeeping.

Made of two separate sheets of copper, rolled up and oxidized right through, the contents of the Copper Scroll could only be determined after it had been cut into parallel strips.

The document is mysterious. Is it either a legend from folklore about fictitious treasures or a catalogue of hiding places for real treasures. The formulas and directions are not decodable, thereby hinting at the possibility that the scroll's content is a myth.

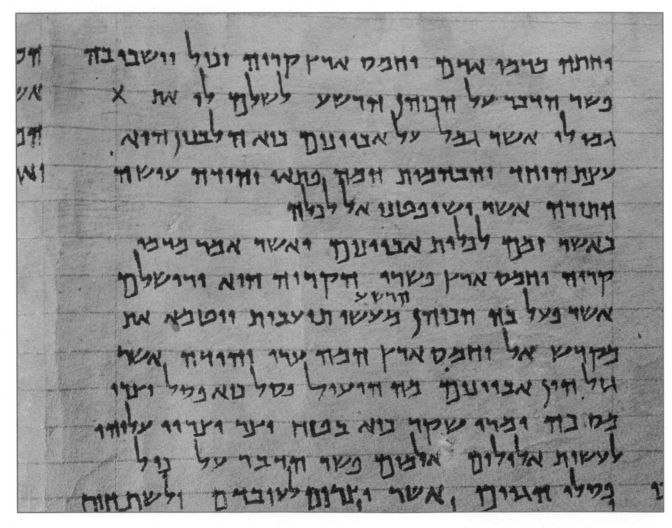

Use this text to draw a treasure map. Your biggest problem is that we don't know where any of the places actually are.

Column I of the Copper Scroll

In the ruin of Horebbah, which is in the valley of Ahor, under the steps heading eastward about forty feet lies a chest of silver that weighs seventeen talents. In the tomb of the third section of stones there are one hundred gold bars. Nine hundred talents are concealed by sediment toward the upper opening, at the bottom of the big cistern in the courtyard of the peristyle (a series of columns surrounding a building or enclosing a court). Priests' garments and flasks that were given as vows are buried in the hill of Kohlit. The opening is at the edge of the canal on its northern side six cubits toward the immersed pool. Enter into the hole of the waterproofed Reservoir of Manos; descend to the left. Forty talents of silver lie three cubits from the bottom.

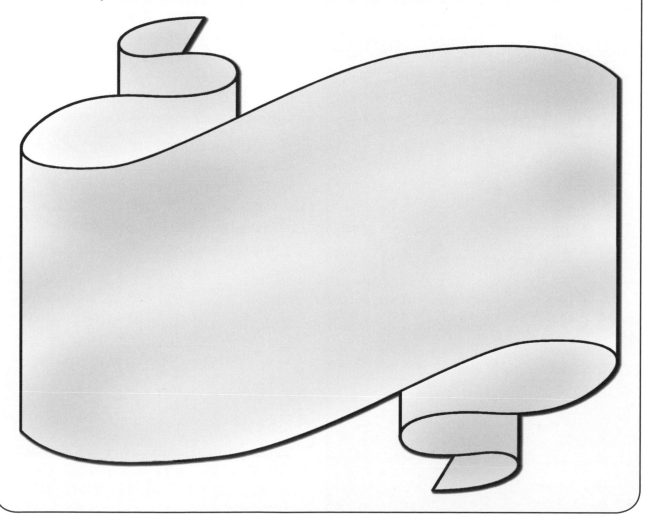

Ein Gedi

Ein Gedi means "the spring of young goats." It is an oasis located west of the Dead Sea, between Masada and the caves of Qumran. It is known for caves, springs, and all kinds of flora and fauna. A kibbutz founded in 1956 is located about a kilometer from the oasis. It offers various tourist attractions and takes advantage of the local weather and the abundance of natural water to grow out-of-season produce.

Ein Gedi National Park

Ein Gedi National Park was founded in 1972 and is one of the most important nature reserves in Israel. The park covers an area of 6,250 acres. The elevation of the land ranges from the level of the Dead Sea, 1,371 feet below sea level, to the plateau of the Judean Desert at 200 meters above sea level.

The park includes two spring-fed streams with flowing water year-round: Nahal David and Nahal Arugot. Two other springs, the Shulamit and Ein Gedi springs, also flow in the reserve. The springs generate approximately three million cubic meters of water per year. Much of the water is used for agriculture or bottled for drinking.

The kibbutz area contains an internationally acclaimed botanical garden. There one can find more than 900 species of plants from all over the world.

History

The oldest archaeological finds at Ein Gedi include a temple and hundreds of copper and ivory ceremonial vessels dating from the

Chalcolithic period (4000 years B.C.E.). The remains of a pool and living quarters indicate that members of the Essene sect may have inhabited the area above Ein Gedi during the first century C.E.

This period of Jewish habitation lasted on and off for 700 years, until the end of the Byzantine empire around 550 C.E, when the settlement was destroyed by fire and abandoned. Ein Gedi was developed extensively during this time, and the remains of agricultural terraces, cisterns, and aqueducts can still be seen.

The ruins of an ornate synagogue dating from the Byzantine era and mosaics with Hebrew and Aramaic inscriptions have been extensively restored and can be viewed in Ein Gedi National Park.

In April 1849 Captain William Lynch led an American expedition down the Jordan River. When he "discovered" Ein Gedi he renamed it George Washington Spring.

The Shachars Hiking through Ein Gedi
(http://tiny.cc/7px06)

Ibex at Ein Gedi

29

Two Versions of the Same Story

Here are two versions of more or less the same story. Both of them tell the story of David hiding from King Saul. The first comes from the Bible; the second is a midrash. Read and compare them.

David and Saul

When Saul returned from chasing the Philistines he was told, "David is in the wilderness of Ein Gedi." Then Saul took three thousand chosen men out of all Israel and went to seek David and his men in front of the rocks of the wild goats. And he came to the sheep's pen by the way, where there was a cave; and Saul went in to relieve himself. Now David and his men were sitting in the innermost parts of the cave.

And the men of David said to him, "Here is the day of which the Eternal said to you, 'Behold, I will give your enemy into your hand, and you shall do to him as it shall seem good to you.'"

Then David arose and stealthily cut off the skirt of Saul's robe. And afterward David's heart killed him, because he had cut off Saul's skirt. He said to his men, "The Eternal forbid that I should do this thing to my lord, the Eternal's anointed, to put forth my hand against him."

So David persuaded his men with these words, and did not permit them to attack Saul. And Saul rose up and left the cave, and went upon his way. Afterward David also arose, and went out of the cave, and called after Saul, "My lord the king!" And when Saul looked behind him, David bowed with his face to the earth. And David said to Saul, "Why do you listen to the words of men who say, 'Behold, David seeks your hurt'? This day your eyes have seen how the Eternal gave you today into my hand in the cave; and some bade me kill you, but I spared you. I said, 'I will not put forth my hand against my lord; for he is the Eternal's anointed.'"

[1 Samuel 24]

30

David and the Spider

When King David was still a boy watching over his father's sheep, he often watched the spiders weave wonderful webs. But he could see no use for spiders. David decided to ask God about it. "Why, Creator of the Cosmos, did you make spiders? You can't even wear their webs as clothing!"

God answered David, "A day will come when you will need the work of this creature. Then you will thank me."

David grew up and became a brave warrior. He defeated the giant Goliath and many enemies of the people of Israel. He married King Saul's daughter and the people adored him as the greatest man in the land. King Saul was jealous and afraid of David and sent his soldiers to kill him. David ran away to the wilderness. He hoped King Saul's fit of anger would pass and he would be safe to return. But King Saul's men kept chasing him.

When the soldiers were very close, David hid in a cave. He heard the footsteps of the men and knew that they would soon find him. David was afraid.

Then David saw a big spider at the front of the cave. Very quickly, it was spinning a web all the way across the opening. Just before the soldiers came up the spider finished the web. As the men started to enter the cave, they ran into the web. "Look," they said, "this web is unbroken. If David were here, he'd have torn the web to pieces. He must be hiding somewhere else. Let's go!"

So because of the spider, David's life was saved. David understood and thanked God for creating all the creatures, including the spiders. (Alphabet of Ben Sira 24b)

1. How are the stories similar?
2. How are they different?
3. What is the lesson of the first story?
4. What is the lesson of the second story?

Masada

Masada comes from the Hebrew word *metzudah*, "fortress." It is the name for a site of ancient palaces and fortifications on top of an isolated rock plateau on the eastern edge of the Judean Desert overlooking the Dead Sea. Masada became famous after the First Jewish-Roman War when a siege of the fortress by troops of the Roman Empire led to a mass suicide of the site's Sicarii (Jewish rebels).

History

According to Josephus, a first-century Roman Jewish historian, King Herod fortified Masada between 37 and 31 B.C.E. as a hideout for himself in the event of a revolt. In 66 C.E., at the beginning of the First Jewish-Roman War against the Roman Empire, a group of Judaic extremist rebels called the Sicarii took Masada from the Roman garrison stationed there.

The Sicarii on Masada were commanded by Elazar ben Ya'ir, and in 70 they were joined by additional Sicarii and their families that were expelled from Jerusalem. For the next two years the Sicarii used Masada as their base for raiding and pillaging. Archaeology indicates that they modified some of the structures they found there. This includes a building that was rebuilt into a synagogue facing Jerusalem. Remains of two *mikva'ot* (ritual baths) were found elsewhere on Masada.

In 72 C.E. the Roman governor of Judaea, Lucius Flavus Silva, marched against Masada and laid siege to the fortress. After failed attempts to breach the wall they built a wall surrounding the mountain and then a ramp against the western face of the plateau using thousands of tons of stones and beaten earth.

The ramp was complete in the spring of 73, and after approximately two to three months of siege, the Romans finally breached the wall. When they entered the fortress the Romans discovered that its 936 inhabitants had set all the buildings but the food storerooms ablaze and committed mass suicide rather than face certain capture.

The storerooms were apparently left standing to show that the defenders retained the ability to live and chose their death over slavery.

Excavating Masada

The site of Masada was identified in 1842 and later excavated between 1963 and 1965 by Yigael Yadin. The original way up to the plateau was an ancient twisting path called the snake path. Today a pair of cable cars now carry those visitors who do not wish to climb. Due to the remoteness and its arid environment the site has remained largely untouched by humans or nature during the past two millennia. Many of the ancient buildings have been restored from their remains, as have the wall paintings of Herod's two main palaces and the Roman-style bathhouses that he built. The synagogue, storehouses,

Yigael Yadin

Yigael Yadin (1917–1984), born in Jerusalem, joined the Haganah in 1933, helped devise many of the strategies employed in the War of Independence. He won the Israel Prize in Jewish Studies in 1956 for his dissertation on research into one of the Dead Sea Scrolls. Yadin's archaeological fieldwork in the fifties and sixties included excavations at Hazor, caves of the Judean Desert, Masada, and Megiddo. He was also instrumental in securing the Dead Sea Scrolls for Israel and decoding a number of the actual scrolls. In his later years he returned to politics. In 1976 he formed a political party called Dash (Democratic Movement for Change), that was a party dedicated to electoral reform. He served as assistant to the prime minister from 1977 to 1981, when he retired from public life to do research full-time. He died in 1984.

1. What is Yigael Yadin's connection to the Dead Sea Scrolls?
2. Write a one sentence obituary of Yigael Yadin.

and houses of the Jewish rebels have also been identified and restored. The meter-high wall that the Romans built around Masada can be seen, together with eleven barracks for the Roman soldiers just outside this wall. Water cisterns two-thirds of the way up the cliff drain the nearby wadis (impressions in the rock) by an elaborate system of channels, which explains how the rebels managed to have enough water for such a long time.

Masada has been a UNESCO World Heritage Site since 2001. An audiovisual light show is presented nightly on the western side of the mountain. In 2007 a new museum opened at the site in which archaeological findings are displayed within a theatrical setting.

Excavations at Masada

Masada
(http://tiny.cc/lg22i)

Elazar Ben Yair's Final Speech

Synagogue at Masada

In Josephus' *The Jewish Wars* he tells the story of Masada. Included in the book is the final speech given by Elazar Ben Yair, the leader of the Sicarii, before his people committed suicide. While Josephus reports that two old women survived the siege, the speech was probably written by Josephus (something historians did in those days). Read the speech and see if you can understand the Sicarii.

Brave and loyal followers! Long ago we resolved to serve neither the Romans nor any other than God, Who alone is the true and just Ruler of humanity. The time has now come that bids us prove our determination by our deeds. At such a time we must not disgrace ourselves. We have never submitted to slavery, even when it brought no danger with it. We must not choose slavery now, and with it penalties that will mean the end of everything if we fall alive into the hands of the Romans. For we were first to revolt, and shall be the last to break off the struggle.

Let our wives die unabused, our children without knowledge of slavery. After that, let us do each other an ungrudging kindness, preserving our freedom as a glorious winding sheet. But first, let our possessions and the whole fortress go up in flames. It will be a bitter blow to the Romans, that I know, to find our persons beyond their reach and nothing left for them to loot. One thing only let us spare—our store of food; it will bear witness when we are dead to the fact that we perished, not through want but because, as we resolved at the beginning, we chose death rather than slavery.

Come! While our hands are free and can hold a sword, let them do a noble service! Let us die unenslaved by our enemies, and leave this world as free men in company with our wives and children.

1. What is Elazar ben Yair's plan?
2. What reasons does he give for their committing suicide?
3. Suicide is against Jewish law. Do you think that the Sicarii on Masada did the right or wrong thing? Why?

Floating in the Dead Sea

The Dead Sea is the lowest point on earth and the second-saltiest lake in the world— eight times saltier than the ocean! The unusually high salt content of the lake allows people to float like buoys, and the rich mineral content is supposed to be good for your skin. Accordingly, many cosmetic companies, like the famous Ahava company, market mineral products from the Dead Sea. At the Dead Sea it is a common practice to cover your body with mineral-rich mud and then dive in the salty water to wash it off— and float! It is salty enough that you can both float and read a newspaper at the same time. Afterward you need to rinse off with fresh water.

Four Other Things to Do Near the Dead Sea

Ahavah Visitors Center. A cosmetic and health products plant using the natural resources of the Dead Sea, with showroom, information center, and tourist shop.

Kalia Beach. A water amusement park with swimming pools, water slides and an aquatic sports center with the largest go-kart track in Israel.

Ein Feshka (*Enot Zukim*). A nature reserve and recreation spot on the Dead Sea shore with facilities for bathing in the rich mineral waters of the lowest lake on earth. Pools and streams are part of the environment.

Metzoke Dragot. This is a visitor center with desert tours, rappelling, and rock-climbing courses. It has a guest house and a restaurant.

CHALLENGE FOR ISRAEL

ISRAELI ARABS

Twenty percent of Israel's citizens are Arab. This does not include those who live in the Palestinian territories of Gaza and the West Bank. Israeli Arabs vote. There are Israeli Arab political parties, Arab members of Knesset (parliament), Arab ministers in the cabinet, and even an Arab member of the Israeli Supreme Court.

But not all things in Israel are equal. There are gaps between the Jewish and Arab populations in Israel. These can be found in hiring and income levels, in schooling, in access to health care, and in town budgets, as well as in proportional representation in the Knesset, ministries, and government posts.

There is a high dropout rate among Arab students. In addition, while 86.6% of Jewish students passed their graduation exams in 2000, only 70.4% of Arab students who lasted in school to graduation passed the test.

About one-half of all Arab families in Israel live under the poverty line (49.9% in 2004). According to the *New York Times*, "a recent report on poverty published last year by Israel's National Insurance Institute indicated that 53 percent of the impoverished families in Israel are Arabs."

The main problem is that on the one hand, democracies need to uphold the full and equal rights of all citizens; on the other hand, Israel is a Jewish state. As a Jewish state, its main purpose is to provide a sovereign homeland for Jews from around the world. Maintaining this political contradiction—a state that is both Jewish and democratic—requires constant balancing. When it comes to its own Arab population, the State of Israel has work to do.

Haifa

חֵיפָה

H

Haifa is the largest city in northern Israel and the third-largest city in the country. The city is a seaport located on Israel's Mediterranean coastline in Haifa Bay. It is one of the country's major industrial centers. Haifa is sort of the San Francisco of Israel.

An Island of Tolerance

Haifa is probably Israel's most progressive city. It has always had a large Arab population, and today Haifa is one of the few places in Israel where Jews and Arabs are in regular contact and make genuine efforts to promote coexistence. Beit ha-Gefen is one of the organizations that run programs for Jews and Arabs there.

Other minorities have also found Haifa a comfortable place to live. In fact, it is the world headquarters for the Baha'i Faith, whose spectacular golden-domed shrine of the Báb is one of the city's landmarks. The city also has a reputation for having a more pluralist approach to Judaism. It is one of a few big cities in Israel where the buses run on Shabbat and where many businesses stay open.

Haifa, Israel Wikipedia travel guide video (http://tiny.cc/273bs)

Beit Hagefen—to Live in Peace
(http://tiny.cc/ll2qm)

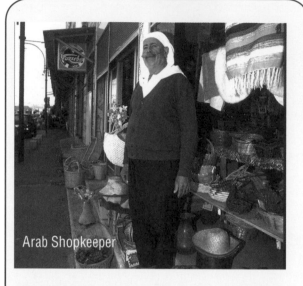

Arab Shopkeeper

Programming Beit ha-Gefen

On this page you learned about Beit ha-Gefen, an Arab-Jewish cultural center in <u>H</u>aifa. Among the things they do is run programs for 5th–11th graders from Jewish, Muslim, and Christian backgrounds.

Imagine that your class was going to take part in a program with Muslim and Christian classes. What would you have the group do? Program three ninety-minute sessions.

1._____

_____

2._____

_____

3._____

_____

Beit ha-Gefen

Beit ha-Gefen was founded in 1963 to create a place for social and cultural meetings between Jews and Arabs and to encourage understanding and coexistence. Beit ha-Gefen sponsors a wide range of activities for both Arabs and Jews, including cross-cultural gatherings for all age groups, extracurricular activities, women's clubs, an Arabic theater, a Visitors Center, an Arab/Jewish folklore troupe, a library, an art gallery, and a training center for Education for Democracy and Coexistence.

How <u>H</u>aifa Is Put Together

<u>H</u>aifa from port

<u>H</u>aifa is built on the side of Mount Carmel, where Elijah defeated the pagan priests of Baal. In the third century C.E. <u>H</u>aifa was a dye-making center. Its main product was the blue thread once used in wrapping the fringes on a tallit. Today it is home to two world-class academic institutions, the University of <u>H</u>aifa and the Technion—The Israel Institute of Technology. High-tech companies such as Intel, IBM, Microsoft, Motorola, and Google have opened branches in <u>H</u>aifa.

40

The city of Haifa is divided into three topographical levels. The lower city, the *Namal,* is the commercial center with modern port facilities. In Hebrew נָמֵל *Namal* means port. The middle level, *Hadar,* is an older residential area, and the upper level, *Har ha-Carmel,* consists of modern neighborhoods overlooking the sandy beaches of Haifa Bay. Israel's only subway, the *Carmelit,* connects the upper and lower city. Many neighborhoods are connected by long flights of stairs.

The city has a population of about 267,800 people. Ninety percent of the population are Israeli Jews. Nine percent of Haifa's population are Arab, The majority of the Arabs live in the Arab neighborhoods Wadi Nisna, Abbas, and Halisa.

The History of Haifa

Unlike Tel Aviv, Haifa is a very old city. It is first mentioned in the Talmud around the third century C.E. as a small town and a center for making the traditional *tekhelet* dye used for the blue/purple thread on a tallit. The archaeological site of Shikmona lies southwest of the modern Bat Galim neighborhood. The Byzatines ruled there until the seventh century, when the city was conquered—first by the Persians, then by the Arabs. In 1100 it was conquered by the Crusaders. The Muslim Mameluks captured it in 1265.

In 1761 Daher El-Omer, Bedouin ruler of Akko and the Galilee, destroyed and rebuilt the town in a new location, surrounding it with a wall. After El-Omar's death in 1775 the town remained under Ottoman rule until 1918.

The Old City of Akko

41

Muhamed Assad

My name is Muhamed. Muhamed is both a Muslim name and an Israeli name because I am an Israeli Arab. I am an Arab and I am a citizen of Israel. My parents pay Israeli taxes and vote in Israeli elections. I am just like any other Israeli child. I go to school, play sports, and watch television. The only difference is, when I finish high school I will not have to go into the Israeli army.

Many of the foods that Israelis like are really Arab foods. Pita, falafel, shishkabob, swarma and other things you can buy and eat on the street were first made by my ancestors. One of the best things my mother makes is sesame lamb meatballs with minted yogurt dip.

My favorite sport is football, which Americans call soccer. I play on a team and I am a forward. My favorite team is the team from the village of Sakhnin. They are a team that comes from an Arab village in Israel.

I study both Hebrew and Arabic. I speak both but at home my family speaks Arabic. My parents do not agree with everything Israel does. They regularly vote for an Arab political party that disagrees with Israel, too. Disagreeing with what the government is doing is something that is allowed in a democracy and Israel is a democracy.

Akko

Slowly Akko, the ancient city, began to decline while Haifa, the modern industrial city, grew in importance. The German Templars arrived in 1868 and settled in what is now known as the German Colony of Haifa. The Templars played a major role in commerce and industry and helped to modernize the city.

In the 20th century Haifa emerged as an industrial port city, and the Hejaz railway and the Technion were established. The Jewish population increased steadily with immigration from Europe, so that by 1945 the population had shifted to 33% Muslim, 20% Christian, and 47% Jewish.

The Druze Villages

The Druze villages just next door to Haifa are Dalyat el-Carmel and Ossefiya. They offer a firsthand experience of Druze culture. The colorful marketplace of Dalyat el-Carmel provides Druze handwork and craftwork and traditional foods such as Druze pitas.

Ossefiya is famous for its Arab Bedouin Heritage Center, known as Albadia. Here you will be welcomed with Bedouin hospitality and traditional food and stories from traditional Bedouin religion and history, and you will be able to visit the traditional workshops as well.

Meet the Druze

The Druze community in Israel is officially recognized as a separate religious entity with its own courts (with authority in matters of personal status, marriage, divorce, and adoption) and spiritual leadership. Their culture is Arab and their language Arabic, but in 1948 they opted against Arab nationalism and have since served (first as volunteers, later within the draft system) in the Israeli Defense Forces (IDF) and the Border Police.

The Druze consider their faith to be a new interpretation of the three monotheistic religions, Judaism, Christianity, and Islam. In their understanding Adam was not the first human being, but the first person to believe in one God. Their mentors and prophets come from all three religions and include Jethro and Moses, John the Baptist and Jesus, Salman the Persian, and Mohammed.

The Druze religion is secret and closed to converts. Druze are forbidden to eat pork, smoke, or drink alcohol.

Faith in the Holy Land—the Druze Community (http://tiny.cc/kucgm)

43

The Baha'i World Center

Haifa's most impressive sightseeing attraction is the Baha'i Shrine and Gardens. The Baha'i gardens with their stone peacocks and eagles and delicately manicured cypress trees are a restful, beautiful memorial to the founders of the Baha'i faith. Haifa is the international headquarters for the Baha'i faith.

Baha'is believe in the unity of all religions and see all religious leaders—Christ, Buddha, Muhammad, Moses—as messengers of God who were sent at different times in history. The most recent of these heavenly teachers, according to Baha'is, was Baha' Allah. He was exiled by the Turkish authorities to Akko, wrote his doctrines there, and died a peaceful death in Bahji House just north of Akko.

In the Haifa gardens the huge gold-domed shrine is the tomb of the Bab. He came before Baha' Allah to prepare the way. The tomb is a sight to see, with ornamental goldwork and flowers in almost every nook and cranny.

On a higher hilltop looking like the Parthenon in Greece stands the Baha'i International Archives building and the Universal House of Justice, with fifty-eight marble columns and hanging gardens behind.

The Baha'i Faith

Universal House of Justice

The **Baha'i Faith** emphasizes the spiritual unity of all humankind. There are around six million Baha'is in more than 200 countries and territories around the world. The Baha'i writings describe a single, indestructable God, the creator of all things, including all the creatures and forces in the universe. Baha'i teachings state that God is too great for humans to fully comprehend by themselves. Human understanding of God comes through revelation.

The Baha'i writings emphasize the equality of all human beings and the abolition of prejudice. Humanity is seen as one, though having a diversity of races and cultures is seen as worthy of appreciation and tolerance. Doctrines of racism, nationalism, caste, and social class are seen as artificial barriers to unity. The Baha'i teachings state that the unification of humankind is the most important issue in the the present world.

A Word About Islam

Islam is usually translated by Muslim scholars as "submission". But it specifically means a *peaceful* submission to the will of Allah, or God, a submission that brings *peace* to the believer. A Muslim is a person who accepts the beliefs of Islam, who peacefully submits to the will of Allah, and follows the teachings, traditions and practices first developed by Mohammed, the primary prophet of Islam.

These teachings of Mohammed were first written in the Qu'ran, the holy book of Islam, supposedly dictated to him by the angel Gabriel. Mohammed lived from 570 C.E. to 632 C.E. He was born in the Muslim holy city of Mecca in the southern part of Saudi Arabia.

Today more than one billion Muslims are scattered throughout the world. Contrary to what most of you probably think, a very large percentage of Muslims live outside of the Middle East, speak little if any Arabic and live relatively normal lives within their various countries. The largest population of Muslims lives in Indonesia.

Any observant, devout Muslim will tell you that all of Islam is summarized and contained within its' Shahada. It is spoken in Arabic: "*Ilaha illa Allah. Muhammad rasul Allah*", and it translates as "**There is no god but Allah. Muhammed is the messenger of God**." Saying these words (and meaning them) is what makes a Muslim a Muslim.

Hatikvah

As long as in the heart, within,

A Jewish soul still yearns,

And onward toward the East,

An eye still watches toward Zion.

Our hope has not yet been lost,

The two-thousand-year-old hope,

To be a free nation in our own homeland,

The land of Zion and Jerusalem.

כָּל עוֹד בַּלֵּבָב פְּנִימָה

נֶפֶשׁ יְהוּדִי הוֹמִיָּה.

וּלְפַאֲתֵי מִזְרָח קָדִימָה

עַיִן לְצִיּוֹן צוֹפִיָּה.

עוֹד לֹא אָבְדָה תִּקְוָתֵנוּ.

הַתִּקְוָה בַּת שְׁנוֹת אַלְפַּיִם.

לִהְיוֹת עַם חָפְשִׁי בְּאַרְצֵנוּ

אֶרֶץ צִיּוֹן וִירוּשָׁלַיִם.

Hatikvah, "The Hope", is the national anthem of Israel. Its text was written by Naftali Herz Imber, a Jew from Galacia, Poland who moved to Palestine in the early 1880s. The anthem's underlying message is about hope, the wish of the Zionists that they might someday attain national independence in the Land of Israel.

1. What about *Hatikvah* makes it a good national anthem for a Jewish state?

2. *Hatikvah* was the unofficial anthem of the State of Israel from the time the State was created. In 2004 it was made the official anthem. At that time there was a big debate in Knesset (Parliament) as to whether it should be chosen. Some members of the Knesset said that it is unfair to Muslim, Christian, Druze, and other non—Jewish citizens of Israel. What makes *Hatikvah* a problem for them?

3. Do you think *Hatikvah* is a good national anthem for Israel? Why? Why not?

Hatikvah (http://tinyurl.com/cgbyler)

Five Other Places to Visit in and around <u>H</u>aifa

Ein Hod. The artist's village of

Ein Hod attracts many tourists. It was established in 1953 by Marcel Janco, a leading artist of the Dada movement. It overlooks the Mediterranean coast and the Crusader castle of Atlit.

During the summer months Ein Hod hosts performances of popular music.

Mount Carmel National Park.

Carmel ridge is a great place to study nature and history. Over 250 sites inhabited by prehistoric human beings have been identified in the area, dating back 500,000 years. A significant finding from 100,000 years ago was that this area was inhabited by two groups with very different physical characteristics. A population of Neanderthals lived no more than 300 meters from a population of modern human beings.

Atlit: The Museum of Illegal Immigration. During most of their

mandate in Israel, the British restricted Jewish immigration. Right after the Holocaust the British blocked Jewish immigration. Jews attempted to reach Israel illegally. The British opened detention camps for those who were caught. The largest of the detention camps was Atlit, south of <u>H</u>aifa. The Atlit detention camp has been rebuilt and is being developed as a museum of the illegal immigration.

Port of <u>H</u>aifa

Akko (Acre in Crusader times) is one of the most ancient ports in the world. It is full of attractive historical and archaeological sites. These include the Al Jazzar Mosque, the Knights' Halls (named after the Hospitallers), the Pasha Turkish Bath House, the Khan El Umdan (the Inn of the Columns), and the Underground Museum, which commemorates the underground prisoners from the British Mandate period.

Rosh ha-Nikrah. The cliff known as Rosh ha-Nikrah is the most northerly point on the Israeli coast. It is especially well known for the crevices that have formed in its rocks due to the waves of the sea pounding against the limestone cliff. These crevices have been carved out naturally into caves and tunnels. A cable car descends from the top of the cliff down to the bottom.

Haifa Time Line. Make a timeline with these people on it.

- Elijah 850 B.C.E.
- *Aliyah Bet* person 1947 C.E.
- First human on Mt. Carmel 500,000 B.C.E.
- Neanderthal remains 100,000 B.C.E.
- Carmelite monks 1190 C.E.
- Baha' Allah d. 1892 C.E.
- Druze beginnings (first report) 1167 C.E.
- Muhammad d. 632 C.E.
- Jewish *T'khellet* Dyer 250 C.E.
- Yona Yahav, mayor of Haifa, 2008

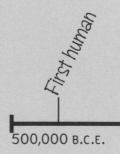

First human

500,000 B.C.E.

Rose Warfman

Aliyah Bet was the second major wave of Jewish immigration to Palestine before the State of Israel was declared. The British quotas made it difficult for Jews escaping Nazi persecution to flee to Israel. Most had to do it "illegally." One of the famous ships of Jewish illegal immigrants was the *Exodus*. Rose Warfman was born in Zurich, a member of the French Resistance, and was the one who falsified the papers that let the *Exodus* leave port and try for Palestine. The story of this ship is famous because its passengers were sent away from the shores of Palestine by the British. When they returned to France in three different ships they refused to disembark and return to Europe. They were redirected to Hamburg and forced off the ships to return to displaced persons camps in Germany. The story of *the Exodus* caused an international uproar and convinced the world that the British were incapable of properly managing Palestine. Rose never lived in Israel but helped people get there.

1. Why do you think Rose Warfman helped the Exodus if she wasn't planning on making *aliyah* to Israel?

2. Why did so many Jews break the law in order to get to *Eretz Yisrael*?

Yona Yahav

2008 C.E.

New Jerusalem

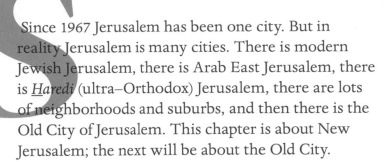

Since 1967 Jerusalem has been one city. But in reality Jerusalem is many cities. There is modern Jewish Jerusalem, there is Arab East Jerusalem, there is _Haredi_ (ultra–Orthodox) Jerusalem, there are lots of neighborhoods and suburbs, and then there is the Old City of Jerusalem. This chapter is about New Jerusalem; the next will be about the Old City.

Jerusalem is both the capital city and the largest city in Israel. It has a population of one million. Located in the Judean Mountains, the city has a history that goes back as to 5,000 B.C.E. It one of the oldest cities in the world. Jerusalem is the holiest city in Judaism and the spiritual center of the Jewish people since the 10th century B.C.E. The city contains a number of significant Christian sites and is considered the third holiest city in Islam. The walled area of Jerusalem, which was the entire city until the 1860s, is now called the Old City.

Modern Jerusalem has grown up around the Old City. The Arab population resides in clusters in the north, east, and south. Today Jerusalem remains a point of argument in the Israeli-Palestinian Conflict. After the Six-Day War, Israel annexed East Jerusalem and unified the city.

In May 2006 65% of those who lived in Jerusalem were Jewish, 32% were Muslim, and 2% were Christian. These different populations live and work apart from each other.

Jerusalem sort of glows because of the special stone used in constructing every building. It is a rule that all buildings be constructed of Jerusalem stone (dolomitic limestone) in order to preserve the unique historic and aesthetic character of the city.

Jerusalem of Gold—Yerushalayim shel Zahav—Ofra Haza (http://tiny.cc/rrazi)

51

Capital of Israel

On December 5, 1949, the State of Israel's first Prime Minister, David Ben-Gurion, proclaimed Jerusalem as Israel's capital. All branches of Israeli government are there: the Knesset, the Supreme Court, and both the President and Prime Minister.

Knesset

The Knesset is Israel's legislature. The Knesset got its name and size, 120, from the *Knesset ha-Gedolah* (Great Assembly), the council convened in Jerusalem by Ezra and Nehemiah in the 5th century B.C.E. The Hebrew word כְּנֶסֶת *Knesset* comes from לְכַנֵּס *l'khanes* "to gather."

Israeli politics are complicated. To begin with, there are usually fifteen to twenty different political parties at any given time. Each party puts up a list of candidates for the Knesset. Israeli voters vote for a party. The percentage of votes a party gets

represents the number of seats the party gets in the Knesset. So a party that gets 10% of the vote gets twelve seats, and the top twelve names on their list will enter Knesset.

Members of Knesset (MKs) are elected every four years unless early elections are called. The Knesset enacts and revises laws.

How the Knesset Works

Israel is a parliamentary democracy. Israel's democracy is made up of legislative, executive, and judicial branches. The Knesset is where new laws are introduced and passed.

Like the Prime Minister of Britain, the Prime Minister of Israel is determined in each election by which of the political parties gets the most votes. The political parties that compete for election to the Knesset reflect a wide range of outlooks and beliefs. There is a high level of participation in elections to the Knesset—77% to 87% of eligible voters take part. There are between ten and fifteen parties represented.

The party with the most votes must form a coalition with other parties in order to create a government.

Proposed bills are considered by appropriate committees and go through three readings before being voted on by the Knesset. Any number of Knesset members present constitutes a quorum, and a simple majority of those present is required for passage. The Knesset meets weekly to consider items on its agenda, debate, and vote to pass new laws. But it does not convene on Fridays, Saturdays, and Sundays in deference to its Muslim, Jewish, and Christian members. While the official language of the Knesset is Hebrew, Arab members may address the legislature in Arabic, with simultaneous translation provided, because Arabic is the second official language of the State of Israel.

The Knesset

53

Kobi Kahn and Shira Friedman

We are Kobi Kahn and Shira Friedman. Kobi is short for Ya'akov (Jacob). Shira means song and isn't short for anything. Kobi's family made *aliyah* to Jerusalem from London. Shira's made *aliyah* from New Jersey. We both go to the Tali school on French Hill. In Israel there are two kinds of public schools. One kind is Orthodox and the other kind is Secular. The Tali schools are a third kind. They were started by parents, most of them North American immigrants from Conservative or Reform backgrounds, who sought to offer their children a serious pluralistic Jewish education within non-Orthodox state schools.

Kobi's family goes to a *Masorti* synagogue. *Masorti* is the Israeli name for its Conservative movement. Shira's family goes to a Progressive synagogue. Progressive is what Reform Jews call their movement. Our two synagogues are very different from each other but both are even more different from Orthodox synagogues. In our two synagogues men and women sit together and share in leading the service. In Orthodox synagogues there is a division between men and woman and only men lead.

While Shira plays the electric guitar, Kobi plays classical flute. Both of us have the same favorite radio station: *Galgalatz*, that is Israeli Army Radio.

The Prime Minister

The Prime Minister is the head of the Israeli government. The Prime Minister is elected by a majority of the Knesset. In Israel's history, no party has ever won a majority of the the seats in the Knesset. In order to form a government and appoint the prime minister and the other ministers, an Israeli political party needs majority support in the Knesset—61 seats. In order to accomplish that, parties will form a coalition (compromise) with other parties.

The President of Israel (who is himself elected by the Knesset) selects a member of Knesset to take the responsibility and the challenge of putting together a coalition. He can select any Knesset member, but by tradition he selects the chairman of the largest party.

This begins a series of negotiations between the various parties. The chairman of the largest party makes a series of promises to the parties he wants to join the coalition. He can offer posts in his Cabinet—the minister of education or the minister of finance, for example. He can also agree to include aspects of a minority party's platform as part of the coalition's platform.

The President

In England there is the Queen, who is Head of State, and the Prime Minister, who is Head of government. In Israel there is the President, who is head of state, and the Prime Minister, who is head of government (the American president has both roles). The President of the State of Israel, נְשִׂיא הַמְּדִינָה *Nesi Ha-Medina*, is largely a ceremonial figurehead.

Although the president's role is non-political, Israeli heads of state perform important ceremonial and educational functions. Israeli presidents also play a part in the formation of the cabinet or government. They are required to consult leaders of all political parties in the Knesset and to designate a member of the legislature to organize a cabinet.

The president lives in an official residence, בֵּית-הַנָּשִׂיא *Beit ha-Nasi* (the House of the President) and welcomes all foreign dignitaries. Until recently the president would have a sukkah at his home. During Sukkot every Israeli citizen was welcome to come into the President's sukkah, take a picture with him, and talk for a minute or two about any issue that was important to him or her.

The Supreme Court building

The Israeli Supreme Court

The **Supreme Court**, בֵּית-הַמִּשְׁפָּט הָעֶלְיוֹן *Beit ha-Mishpat ha-Elyon,* is the highest layer of the court system in the State of Israel. In Hebrew, עֶלְיוֹן means "supreme." The Supreme Court sits on a hilltop in Jerusalem and covers cases from the entire State. A ruling of the Supreme Court is binding upon every court other than the Supreme Court itself. The Supreme Court is allowed to change its own mind.

The number of Supreme Court justices is decided by the Knesset. Usually twelve justices serve in the Supreme Court. At the present time there are fourteen. At the head of the Supreme Court and at the head of the judicial system as a whole stands the President of the Supreme Court, who is helped by the Deputy President. A judge's term ends at seventy years of age or when he or she resigns, dies, is appointed to another position that is disqualifying, or is removed from office.

Israeli Elections*

Your class is going to try to form an Israeli government.

a. Divide your class into the following political parties. Assign each party the number of seats won in the last election.

b. Pick a president of Israel and have the president assign the leader of the Kadima party (which has the highest total) to form a government.

c. Start negotiating. The head of Kadima can offer ministries to other parties, including Minister of Agriculture and Rural Development; Minister of Communications; Minister of Construction and Housing; Minister of Culture, Sports, Science and Technology; Minister of Education; Minister of the Environment; Minister of Finance; Minister of Health; Minister of Internal Security; Minister of Justice; Minister of National Infrastructure; Minister of Pensioner Affairs; Minister of Tourism; Minister of Welfare

Each card represents a political party.

and Social Services; Minister of Strategic Affairs; Minister of Defense; Minister of Foreign Affairs; Minister of Industry, Trade and Labor; Minister of Transportation; Minister of the Diaspora, Society and Fight Against Antisemitism. Every minister sits on the cabinet, but Kadima should keep the ministries it considers most important for itself.

d. Kadima can also agree to accept or reject policies that other parties think are important.

e. If Kadima can put together a coalition with sixty-one seats, they win. If not, Likkud (with the next highest total) gets a chance to put together a coalition.

f. When a government is organized, the President of Israel announces it.

NOTE: In Israeli politics, right-of-center parties tend to favor hard-line policies toward the Palestinians, retaining all territory captured in the 1967 Six-Day War, and free-market economic policies. Left-of-center parties tend to favor negotiated peace agreements with the Palestinians, relinquishing territory, and economic policies that favor the poor.

* Based on the 2009 elections.

Kadima, **28 seats**. Kadima tries to find policies in between the extremes. Kadima promised to draw Israel's permanent borders within four years by withdrawing from parts of the West Bank.

Likud, **27 seats**. Likud opposed the disengagement and campaigned against further disengagements without Palestinian concessions in exchange. Likud supports free-market economic policies and a hard line against terror.

Yisrael Beiteinu, **15 seats**. This party's appeal was centered in Israel's large Russian immigrant population. Yisrael Beiteinu's platform proposed exchanging Israeli land with heavy Arab Israeli populations for West Bank land with heavy Jewish populations. Also important to Yisrael Beiteinu is civil marriage, because many Russian immigrants are not halakhically (legally) Jewish and thus cannot get married legally.

Labor, **13 seats**. During the first twenty-five years of Israel's history Labor was Israel's dominant party. Labor believes in workers' rights and supports negotiations with the Palestinians. Labor promised voters a major increase in the minimum wage.

Shas, **11 seats**. Shas represents Israel's *Sefardi haredim* (ultra-Orthodox Jews). Its platform includes continued religious control of Jewish marriage and divorce and increased subsidies for its yeshivot and for large families. Shas's rabbinical leadership might support territorial concessions, but the rank-and-file membership of Shas is overwhelmingly against them.

United Torah Judaism, **5 seats**. This is Israel's other *haredi* party, representing Ashkenazi *haredim*. United Torah Judaism strongly opposes civil marriage and supports increased subsidies for its yeshivot and for large families.

United Arab List—Ta'al, **4 seats**. The United Arab List represents the Israeli Arab minority. Because together they represent less than one-tenth of the Knesset, they have little hope of passing legislation or serving in a government led by the Zionist parties. The Arab parties fight for Arab civil rights, including equal funding for Arab schools.

National Union/National Religious Party, 4 seats. This merger of two parties represents Israel's *dati leumi* (national religious) population. Unlike the *haredim*, *dati leumi* Israelis serve in the army and celebrate Israeli Independence Day. The National Union/National Religious Party strongly opposed disengagement.

Hadash, 4 seats. Hadash, an Arab party that was once part of The United Arab List, supports evacuation of all Israeli settlements, a complete withdrawal from the territories, and the establishment of a Palestinian state. It also supports the right of return or compensation for Palestinian refugees.

Meretz, 4 seats. Meretz is Israel's far-left party, supporting causes such as gay marriage, environmentalism, and the rights of Arab Israelis. It supports negotiations with the Palestinians and territorial concessions.

The Jewish Home, 3 seats. The Jewish Home stand for achieving a just, stable peace; protecting workers' rights; developing social services; equality for the Arab population; eradicating ethnic discrimination; defending the concerns of disadvantaged neighborhoods; protecting democratic freedoms; equality; protecting the environment; eradicating weapons of mass destruction.

Balad, 3 seats. Balad describes itself as a democratic progressive national party for the Palestinian citizens of Israel. It opposes the idea of Israel as a solely Jewish state, and supports its recasting as a binational state. Even though it received 3 seats, Balad was disqualified from the 2009 Israeli elections on grounds that it does not recognize the State of Israel and calls for armed conflict against it.

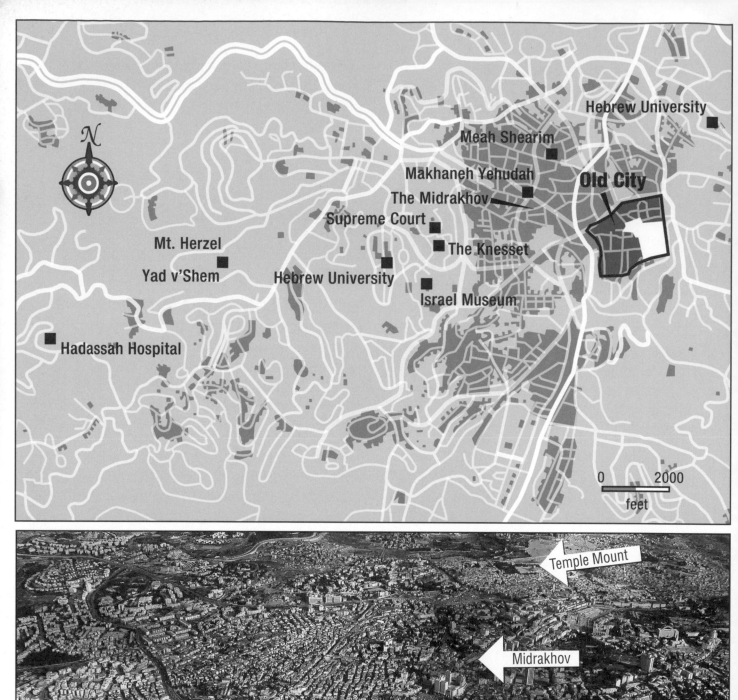

Hebrew University

Meah Shearim

Makhaneh Yehudah

The Midrakhov

Old City

Supreme Court

Mt. Herzel

The Knesset

Yad v'Shem

Hebrew University

Israel Museum

Hadassah Hospital

0   2000
feet

Temple Mount

Midrakhov

Israel Museum

The Israel Museum

On a hill near the Knesset, the Israeli Supreme Court, and the Hebrew University of Jerusalem sits the Israel Museum. It is the national museum of the State of Israel. As Jerusalem's leading art museum, it annually attracts nearly one million visitors, approximately one-third of them from overseas. The twenty-acre museum complex is made up of several buildings. It has an extensive collection of Judaica, archaeological findings, and Israeli and European art. The Dead Sea Scrolls are housed in the museum's Shrine of the Book. The museum has a large outdoor sculpture garden, and a scale model of the Second Temple.

Shrine of the Book

Apply to the Hebrew University

Name_____

Age_____

Address_____

_____

School _____

Hobbies _____

_____

_____

Essay

I want to study in Jerusalem because _____

_____

_____

_____

_____

_____

_____

The Hebrew University of Jerusalem

The Hebrew University is one of Israel's oldest, largest, and most important institutions of higher learning and research. It has two campuses in Jerusalem—one near the Israel Museum and one on Mount Scopus. The Hebrew University developed a world-renowned reputation for its studies in the sciences and in religion, a subject in which it possesses abundant resources, including the world's largest Jewish studies collection. Lots of foreign students spend a semester or a year there.

Mount Herzl and the Military Cemetery

Theodor Herzl's will read: "I wish to be buried in a metal coffin next to my father, and to remain there until the Jewish people will transfer my remains to Eretz Israel." Herzl died a year later and was buried in Vienna. In 1949 Herzl's remains were brought to Israel and reburied in Jerusalem. From then on Mount Herzl has served as the national cemetery where Zionist leaders, the presidents of Israel, prime ministers, and Speakers of the Knesset are laid to rest. On the northern slope of Mount Herzl is the military cemetery of Jerusalem, and to the west is *Yad Vashem*, which commemorates the Holocaust. These three sites together comprise *Har ha-Zikaron* (the Mount of Memory).

Israel's annual memorial day for its fallen soldiers is observed on 2 Iyyar (usually in May), the day before Independence Day. Official ceremonies take place on *Har Herzl*. Here are buried many of Israel's leaders, including its assassinated Prime Minister, Yitzhak Rabin, whose memorial symbolizes the search for peace.

Yad Vashem

Yad Vashem (Holocaust Martyrs' and Heroes' Remembrance Authority) is Israel's official memorial to the victims of the Holocaust, established in 1953 through the Memorial Law passed by the Knesset. The origin of the name is from a Biblical verse: AND TO THEM WILL I GIVE IN MY HOUSE AND WITHIN MY WALLS A יָד וָשֵׁם *YAD VA-SHEM* (A MEMORIAL AND A NAME)...THAT SHALL NOT BE CUT OFF (Isaiah 56.5).

The new Holocaust History Museum was built as a triangular structure. It is 180 meters long, with stark walls made from reinforced concrete. The museum covers an area of more than 4,000 square meters and is mostly situated below ground level. There are ten exhibition halls, each devoted to a different chapter in the history of the Holocaust. The building's triangular architectural shape is

said to represent the bottom half of a Star of David, because the world's Jewish population was cut in half as a result of the Holocaust.

The principal memorial at *Yad Vashem* is the Hall of Remembrance (*Ohel Yizkor*). The severe concrete-walled structure with a low tent-like roof stands empty save for an eternal flame. Engraved in the black basalt floor are the names of twenty-one Nazi extermination camps, concentration camps, and killing sites in Central and Eastern Europe. A crypt in front of the memorial flame contains ashes of victims.

The approach to the Hall of Remembrance is lined with trees planted in honor of non–Jewish men and women—Righteous Among the Nations—who, at the risk of their own lives, attempted to rescue Jews. Several of the trees honor members of the Christian clergy, among them a Franciscan priest in Assisi,

Yad Vashem: Remembering the Past, Shaping the Future (http://tiny.cc/qk6j4)

the bishop of the Greek island of Zakinthos, a Polish nun in Lithuania, and a French Protestant pastor. More than 20,000 persons have been honored with the title Righteous Among the Nations.

Approximately 1.5 million Jewish children perished in the Holocaust. They are specially remembered in the nearby Children's Memorial, an underground cavern in which the flickering flames of memorial candles are reflected in an infinity of tiny lights within the prevailing darkness.

The Valley of the Communities is a 2.5-acre monument that was dug out from the natural bedrock. Engraved on the massive stone walls of the memorial are the names of over five thousand Jewish communities that

were destroyed and of the few that suffered but survived.

The Memorial to the Deportees is an original cattle car that was used to transport thousands of Jews to the death camps. Perched on the edge of an abyss facing the Jerusalem forest, the monument symbolizes both the impending horror and the rebirth that followed the Holocaust.

Sports

The two most popular sports in Jerusalem, and in Israel as a whole, are soccer and basketball. Beitar Jerusalem Football Club is one of the most popular teams in Israel. Jerusalem's other major football team, and one of Beitar's top rivals, is Hapoel Jerusalem Football Club. Whereas Beitar has been Israel State Cup champion five times, Hapoel has only won the Cup once.

In a league dominated by Maccabi Tel Aviv it has yet to

Beitar Yerushalayim

win a championship, but it has won the Israeli Cup three times, and it took the European ULEB Cup in 2004. In basketball, however, Hapoel Jerusalem is higher up on the scale.

Lion around Jerusalem

The lion represents the tribe of Judah, and because of the significance of lion imagery in Jerusalem's history, it was only natural for the lion to become the official emblem of the Eternal City of Jerusalem. In 2002 more than eighty lions were given to artists to decorate and then placed all over the city.

Now decorate your own lion.

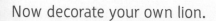

Four Other Places You Should Visit in Jerusalem

Latrun and Mini-Israel.

During the War of Independence the Arab Legion took the police fort at Latrun and used it to cut off traffic between the rest of Israel and Jerusalem. Israel made unsuccessful attempts to take the fort and wound up building a "Burma Road" (around the back way) to get supplies into Jerusalem. In the Six-Day War, Latrun was captured by Israeli forces. Today the fort is known as *Yad la-Shiryon* and includes a museum, a display of over 110 tanks, an amphitheater, an auditorium, a synagogue, and a memorial. Miniature Israel was opened across the street. It features over 350 beautifully crafted exact-replica models of historical, religious, archaeological, and modern sites.

Makhaneh Yehudah is the largest and busiest outdoor market in Israel. It is located in Jerusalem on Yaffo Street. It was established as a neighborhood in 1887 but only became an official market in 1928. Makhaneh Yehudah contains hundreds of stands and shops with vegetables, fruits, fish, meat, baked goods, spices, candy, eggs, cheeses, household appliances, and more accessories.

The Midrahov is an open-air pedestrian mall. Its name is a combination of מִדְרָכָה *midrakhah* (sidewalk) and רְחוֹב *rehov* (street). Cafés have tables out on the cobblestones; vendors display cheap, artsy items like funky jewelry

Golda Meir

Golda Meir (1898–1978) was born Golda Mabovitz in the Ukraine. When she was eight her family moved to the United States, fleeing pogroms. She grew up and was educated in Wisconsin. In 1921 she and her husband Morris made *aliyah* to Israel and joined a kibbutz. On the kibbutz Golda Myerson (she had not yet changed her name) was quickly elected to represent the kibbutz at the Histadrut, the General Federation of Labor. In 1948 she was one of twenty-four signers of Israel's Declaration of Independence, and one of two women.

She would recall, "After I signed, I cried. When I studied American history as a schoolgirl and I read about those who signed the Declaration of Independence, I couldn't imagine these were real people doing something real." She served as Israel's first ambassador to the Soviet Union.

From 1949–1974 she was a member of the Knesset, fulfilling a variety of roles, including Foreign Minister. After the Six-Day War in 1968 she was called out of retirement to serve as Prime Minister. She was the first woman to be elected as head of Israel, and only the third female prime minister ever in the world.

1. What do you think was the thing about Golda Meir that let her be one of the first woman to lead a country?
2. Name some of the important things she did.

and prints; and street musicians are usually out in good weather, playing tunes old and new. It's a great place to sip coffee or munch falafel and watch the passing crowd.

Me'ah She'arim is one of the oldest neighborhoods of Jerusalem. It was established in 1874 as the second settlement outside the walls of the Old City by a building society of one hundred shareholders. The name מֵאָה שְׁעָרִים *Me'ah She'arim* is derived from a verse in Genesis (26:12): Isaac sowed in that land, and in that year he reaped מֵאָה שְׁעָרִים (a hundredfold); God had blessed him.

With its overwhelmingly *Haredi* population, Me'ah She'arim retains the flavor of an East European shtetl. Life revolves around strict adherence to Jewish law, prayer, and the study of Jewish texts.

CHALLENGE FOR ISRAEL

EAST JERUSALEM AND THE WEST BANK

In 1967 East Jerusalem was annexed and put under the control of Israel. In a future peace settlement Palestinians hope to make it their capital. For hundreds of years Arabs have lived in villages throughout East Jerusalem. On the Mount of Olives, in a small Arab village called At-Tur, residents have been taking care of for centuries the Jewish cemetery where sages are buried.

The West Bank is an area conquered and occupied by Israel in 1967. Most of its population is made up of Palestinian Arabs. Since 2005 it has been under the rule of the Palestinian Authority.

There is a security fence between Israel and the West Bank. Some Israelis believe that it keeps Israel safe from terrorism and some believe that it unfairly divides the Arab community from its lands and relatives.

Since Israel declared independence the Arabs rejected the Palestinian state offered to them. There has been continuous unrest in the West Bank. There have been many incursions of the Israeli Army into the West Bank to crack down on violence. The Palestinian Authority gave the Palestinians some level of autonómy (self-government), but with the election of Hamas, a terrorist organization, many questions started to come up: Where is the line between democratically elected leaders and governments and democratic values that support basic freedoms of religion, press, speech, and privacy? Hamas does not recognize the right of Israel to exist. How long do Jews have to be resettled in the land before Arabs realize they are there to stay? How can you make peace with a government that does not recognize you?

In the meantime, independent organizations can continue to do outreach, dialogue, and peace work. Everyone on both sides of the border between the West Bank and Israel can try to lead normal lives. But Israel cannot occupy (control politically) the West Bank forever, and the Palestinians cannot refuse to recognize Israel's right to exist forever.

The Old City of Jerusalem

עִיר הָעַתִּיקָה

The last words in the Passover seder are לְשָׁנָה הַבָּאָה בִּירוּשָׁלַיִם הַבְּנוּיָה *L'shanah ha-Ba'ah b'Yirushalayim ha-B'nuyah,* "Next year in rebuilt Jerusalem." Even at a seder in Israel, even at a seder in Jerusalem the final words are לְשָׁנָה הַבָּאָה בִּירוּשָׁלַיִם הַבְּנוּיָה. The question of why we sing "Next Year in Jerusalem" when we are already in Jerusalem is answered by the word הַבְּנוּיָה *ha-B'nuyah,* "rebuilt." The simple answer is that the kind of building we are talking about is not just physical. In the siddur we find this prayer in the weekday Amidah. It is blessing fourteen.

> And to Jerusalem Your City, may You (God) return in compassion, and may You rebuild it soon in our days as an eternal structure, and may You speedily establish the throne of David within it. Blessed are You, Eternal, the Builder of Jerusalem.

Here we get two difficult ideas. First is the idea that God should return to Jerusalem. That is sort of hard, because if God is everywhere, God is already in Jerusalem. The second problem is "speedily establish the throne of David within it." King David is already dead.

To make sense of this you need to know a few things:

- The Temple was in Jerusalem.
- The Temple was the place where God "lived with Israel." One of its names is *Beit Adonai,* God's house.
- King David was the leader who first conquered Jerusalem for the Jewish people.
- The tradition teaches that a descendent of King David will be the Messiah.

We learn that Jews are looking forward to a time when a third Temple is built in Jerusalem and the Messiah rules the Jewish people. While many many Jews do not want a third Temple and lots of Jews do not believe in a Messiah who is a specific person, Jerusalem remains an important symbol. Jerusalem stands for a world in peace with prosperity for

Jerusalem, The Holy City (http://tiny.cc/v6yt3)
cannot be played on mobile device

69

King David

Considered the great king of Israel, King David is well known and important in the holy books of all three monotheistic religions.

David was born into a peasant family and was a shepherd. The Bible tells us that as a boy he slew the giant Goliath, and grew up to be a major military hero whose power and fame threatened that of Saul, the reigning king. King David unified Judah (the ancient southern province) and Israel (the ancient northern kingdom) and established Jerusalem as capital of the kingdom. David achieved secure borders for Israel by conquering all enemies, and he did much for the unification of the twelve tribes of Israel.

The midrashic tradition has a lot to say about David. When the messiah comes he will be descended from David. The 150 psalms, which form one of the Hebrew Bible's most beautiful and sacred books of poetry, are attributed to King David. That's why so many psalms begin with the words *Mizmor l'David*, a "song of David."

1. What was David's biggest achievement?
2. Why do you think the Midrash connects David to the Messiah?

all. It represents a time when Jews have been a "light to the nations" and people live up to being "created in God's image." Jerusalem is the Jewish symbol that at some point the future will create a better world.

The same idea is found in *Birkat ha-Mazon*, the Grace after Meals.

> Have mercy, O Eternal our God, upon Your people Israel, upon Your city Jerusalem, upon the dwelling place of Your Glory, Zion, upon the rulership of the house of David, Your Messiah, and upon the great and holy House that is called by Your name…Rebuild Jerusalem, the holy city, speedily in our days. Blessed are You, Eternal, Who in mercy rebuilds Jerusalem. Amen.

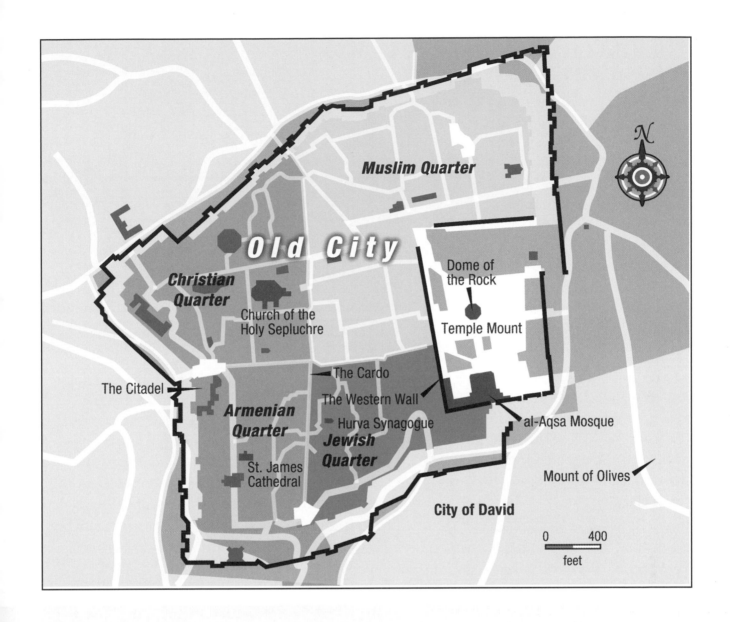

In What Quarter Is Each of the Following Sites?

_____ <u>H</u>urva Synagogue   _____ David's City

_____ Dome of the Rock   _____ The Cardo

_____ Church of the Holy   _____ al-Aqsa Mosque
                 Sepulchre

_____ The Citadel   _____ St. James Cathedral

     _____ The Western Wall

The Old City of Jerusalem

The **Old City** is a .35-square-mile area within the modern city of Jerusalem. Until the 1860s this area constituted the entire city of Jerusalem. The Old City is home to several sites of key religious importance: the Temple Mount and its Western Wall for Jews, the Church of the Holy Sepulchre for Christians, and the Dome of the Rock and al-Aqsa Mosque for Muslims. The Old City is divided into the four quarters—the Muslim Quarter, Christian Quarter, Jewish Quarter, and Armenian Quarter.

Jerusalem is located on the southern spur of a plateau in the Judean Mountains, which include the Mount of Olives (east) and Mount Scopus (northeast). The whole of Jerusalem is surrounded by valleys and wadis (dry riverbeds).

Three of the most prominent valleys in the region—the Kidron, Hinnom, and Tyropoeon valleys—connect just south of the Old City of Jerusalem. The Kidron Valley runs just to the east of the Old City and separates the Mount of Olives from the city proper. Along the southern side of old Jerusalem is the Valley of Hinnom. A third valley starts in the northwest and runs south-southeasterly through the center of the Old City down to the Pool of Siloam. The Temple was built on the fourth side as a way of protecting the city. Three sides had valleys. The fourth side had a mountain with a fort-like Temple.

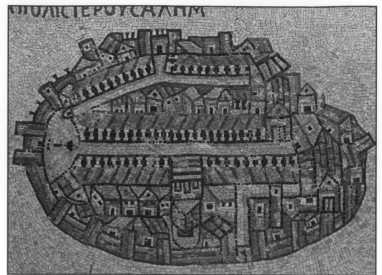

Three Faiths

Jerusalem has been sacred to the Jews since the 10th century B.C.E. as the site of Solomon's Temple and the Second Temple. It is mentioned in the Bible 632 times. Synagogues around the world are traditionally built with the Holy Ark facing Jerusalem, and arks within Jerusalem face the "Holy of Holies." As prescribed in the *Mishnah* and codified in the *Shulḥan Arukh*, daily prayers are recited while facing east toward Jerusalem and the Temple Mount. Many Jews have *Mizraḥ* plaques hung on a wall of their homes to indicate the direction of prayer.

Christianity reveres Jerusalem not only for its role in the Hebrew Bible but also for its significance in the life of Jesus. According to biblical accounts, Jesus was brought to the city of Jerusalem not long after his birth. The site of Jesus' Last Supper is located on Mount Zion. Another prominent Christian site in Jerusalem is Golgotha, the site of the crucifixion.

According to tradition, Jerusalem is the third-holiest city in Islam. It is the location of the place from which Muhammad ascended into heaven and had a vision.

What's in a Name?

Though the city has many names, "Jerusalem" is the most common. Where does the name Jerusalem or, in Hebrew, יְרוּשָׁלַיִם come from?

Here are a few explanations. Examine each of them and answer the questions.

God Named Jerusalem

Why is it called Jerusalem? There are two mentions of Jerusalem in the book of Genesis, but in each the Torah uses a different name.

In Genesis 14 Abraham goes to visit a king/priest named Melkhizedek. Melkhizedek is king of a place called Shalem. Shalem is the first name for the place. In Hebrew it means "complete." In Genesis 14 Melkhizedek feeds Abraham and blesses him.

In Genesis 22 Abraham almost sacrifices Isaac. After the whole ordeal is over Abraham calls the place *Adonai Yireh.* The Torah explains that this means "On the mountain of God there is vision."

Both Abraham and Melkhizedek call God by the name *El Elyon* (Supreme God). Because of this, God combined their names for the place—*Yireh* and *Shalem*—to make the name for the city, *Yerushalayim* [Yehezkel Landau and *Bereshit Rabbah*].

1. According to this explanation, what is special about the city of Jerusalem?
2. According to this explanation, why is Jerusalem a good name for this particular city?

City of Completeness

The name Jerusalem is actually not a Hebrew word. It is originally from a language called Akkadian, which has a lot in common with Hebrew but is much older.

The Akkadian name for the place was *Urušalim*, which means "City of Completeness." The Hebrew word שָׁלֵם, *shalem*, also means "complete."

continued on page 74

73

Why is it called "City of Completeness"? Our rabbis told this story: When God created the world, God needed to start building somewhere. Just as the builder of a house starts by laying a foundation—a really strong platform on which everything else is built—God started the world with a foundation. God ripped a hunk off of God's magnificent throne and hurled it into the *tohu va'vohu*, the chaos that existed before the world. The world was built upon that foundation stone, and when God was done building, the final bits of creation were completed on the same spot where creation started.

Jerusalem is built on that very spot where creation began and ended (*Kohelet Rabbah, Bereshit Rabbah*, and *Zohar*).

> 3. According to this explanation, what is special about the city of Jerusalem?
> 4. According to this explanation, why is Jerusalem a good name for this particular city?

Solomon's City

Jerusalem was first established as a Jewish city when King David conquered it and made it the capital of his kingdom. (That is why another name for Jerusalem is "The City of David".)

King David was not able to complete his capital, however. He built up the city and made himself a palace there, but God would not allow David to build the Temple, because David was a warrior.

The Temple was built by David's son, Solomon. In Hebrew, Solomon is *Shlomo*. The word שָׁלוֹם *shalom* is inside Solomon's name. Solomon was a man of peace, and God instructed him to build the Temple.

When the Temple was built, the city was finally שָׁלֵם, complete (*Kohelet Rabbah*).

> 5. According to this explanation, what is special about the city of Jerusalem?
> 6. According to this explanation, why is Jerusalem a good name for this particular city?
> 7. Why do you think there are so many explanations for the name Jerusalem?

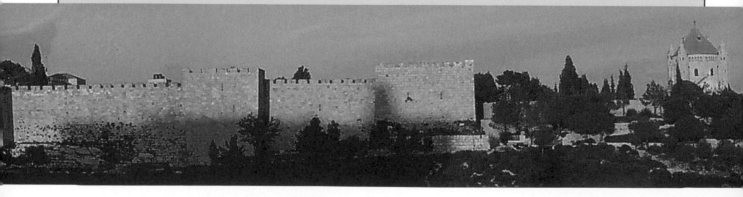

Armenian priests

History

Found pottery suggests that people lived within present-day Jerusalem as far back as the Copper Age, 4,000 B.C.E. The Biblical story says that the Jebusites had control of the city, inhabiting the area around the present-day city until the late 10th century B.C.E., when King David is said to have invaded and conquered their city, making it the capital of the United Kingdom of Israel and Judah around 970 B.C.E.

The Bible describes the city as heavily fortified with a strong wall. The city ruled by King David, known as *Ir David*, the City of David, is now believed to be southwest of the Old City walls, outside the Dung Gate. His son King Solomon extended the city walls. In about 440 B.C.E. Nehemiah returned from Babylon and started the rebuilding of the city.

The current walls of the Old City were built in 1538 by Suleiman the Magnificent. The walls stretch for approximately 2.8 miles and rise to a height of 16–49 feet.

Armenian Quarter

Armenia is a country near Turkey. Armenians have a long and special history in Jerusalem. In 301 C.E., before the Roman Empire made Christianity its official state religion, Armenia was Christian. Their history in Jerusalem began when Jews from Israel and Armenians from Armenia traded with each other in the early centuries C.E. Once the Roman Empire adopted Christianity, Armenian pilgrims were free to buy property and build churches in Jerusalem. From the fourth to eighth centuries C.E. Armenians built about seventy monasteries throughout the Holy

Mary Abbas

My name is Mary. I come from a family of Palestinian Christians that have lived in the same apartment in the Old City of Jerusalem for hundreds of years. I love the Old City and I know every twist and turn in the Christian Quarter where we live. I also work in the Old City helping my father in his spice shop in the *shuk*, the open air market.

My favorite time of year is Easter when our church has these big festivities and the whole Old City is filled with an overflowing of tourists and pilgrims. Everything is so exciting. There are so many special events.

I'm into painting. I love drawing pictures. Sometimes I work with pencils or markers but water color is my favorite. I love the way that the color sinks into the paper. I paint all kinds of sights from around the Old City and love building layers of color. My favorite artist is Monet. I love what he does with light. I try to do the same thing.

I go to a Christian school because most Arab schools are Muslim. We study mathematics, geography, Arabic, Bible and lots of other subjects. What I love so much is that I get to live where the history we study actually happened.

Land. Armenians, unlike the majority of Christians in Israel, are not Arab, but rather are both ethnically and religiously Armenian. During the Crusades, when Christian knights from Europe were on a religious mission to conquer Jerusalem for Christendom, they ransacked Jerusalem. Armenians were seen as separate and different from them. Armenians in Jerusalem were respected under the Muslim rulers and later the Ottoman Empire because of their long history in Jerusalem. Before World War I all of the Middle East was under the control of the Ottoman Empire. Today Israel does its best to safeguard her Armenian minority. Although it is the smallest of the four quarters of the Old City, approximately 1,500 Armenians live there today, many on short-term study programs. It is not uncommon to see Armenian priests clad in ceremonial garb roaming the streets of the Old City.

After the 1948 Arab-Israeli War the four quarters of the city came under Jordanian control. Jordanian law required Armenians and other Christians to give equal time to the Bible and Qur'an in private Christian schools. The 1967 war is remembered by residents of the quarter as a miracle after two unexploded bombs were found inside the Armenian monastery. After the 1967 war the Israeli government gave compensation for repairing any churches or holy sites damaged in the fighting, regardless of who caused the damage. The quarter runs itself as a city within a city (within a city), shutting all gates when night falls.

Things to See in the Armenian Quarter

The Citadel. Now home to the Tower of David Museum of the History of Jerusalem, the Citadel is an imposing fortress inside the city wall beside the Jaffa Gate. It was utilized and expanded throughout the centuries as a means of protection.

St. James Cathedral. This Armenian cathedral is one of the most beautiful of all the sacred buildings in Jerusalem. It was constructed in the 11th and 12th centuries over the traditional tomb of St. James the Apostle. Attending an Armenian Orthodox vespers service is a treat even for non-believers. Vespers is chanted by the seminarians of the Armenian Orthodox seminary across the street from the Cathedral. The chanting is very moving and has a bittersweet tone that is unforgettably beautiful.

St. Mark's Syriac Church. According to tradition, this church was built on the site of the house of Mary, mother of St. Mark. Some historians believe that a small cellar was the true site of the Last Supper.

The Citadel

Church of the Dormition

Church of the Dormition. Adorned by a rounded dome and a tall bell tower, this Mount Zion church is the traditional site of the Virgin Mary's death. Several churches have been built on the site. The present-day structure was built in the early 20th century for the visit of Kaiser Wilhelm II. A statue of the Virgin Mary rests in the crypt surrounded by images of various women listed in the Hebrew Bible.

King David's Tomb. Located on the lower floor of the Crusader building is a small chamber that some believe is King David's tomb. The chamber—divided for separate viewing by men and women—contains a coffin covered by a drape. Today the entrance hall is still used as a synagogue.

Muslim Quarter

The Muslim Quarter is the largest and most populous of the four quarters. It is situated in the northeastern corner of the Old City, extending from the Lion's Gate in the east along the northern wall of the Temple Mount to the south to the Damascus Gate. Walking down the alleyways of the Muslim Quarter, one is witness to many Palestinians of Jerusalem doing their day-to-day shopping for bread, vegetables, spices, clothing, and appliances. Many tourists walk through these covered streets as well—and the shopkeepers are eager for their business. You'll find that almost every alleyway, followed long enough, seems to lead to the Temple Mount, which is where the holiest mosque in Israel is located.

This is also the site of the ancient Jerusalem Temple, so holy to Jews that the chief rabbis of Israel forbid Jews to enter it because only the head priest of ancient days was allowed entrance to the Holy of Holies in the Temple. Now that we no longer know exactly where that is, they think it better to avoid the place entirely. Israeli soldiers guard the entrances to the Temple Mount area.

Things to See in the Muslim Quarter

The Temple Mount. Known in Hebrew as *Har Ha-Bayit,* the Temple Mount is a large rectangular in the southeastern part of the city. This is the site of Solomon's Temple, and later the Second Temple, which was enlarged by Herod the Great and destroyed by the Romans in 70 C.E. It is usually called the Temple Mount. Because the are is also holy to Muslims, the site is extremely controversial, and access is strictly regulated.

The Temple Mount

mosaics, and Arabic calligraphy. The Dome is not a mosque but a shrine whose high ceiling protects a large piece of rock sacred to Muslims, Jews, and Christians. The rock is variously believed to be where Abraham was asked to sacrifice his son Isaac; where Muhammad left the Earth on his Night Journey; and the site of the Holy of Holies of Herod's Temple.

Dome of the Rock. Known in Hebrew as *Kipat ha-Sela* and in Arabic as *Qubbat as-Sakhrah*, the Dome of the Rock is one of the first and most familiar achievements of Islamic architecture. The Dome of the Rock marks the spot from which Muslims believe the Prophet Muhammad ascended to heaven on the back of his fabulous horse before returning to earth to record his vision. The building (together with the neighboring al-Aqsa Mosque) is the third-holiest site in Islam after Mecca and Medina. Built between 687 and 691 C.E. the structure is probably the most spectacular building in the Old City. It is topped with a golden dome visible from afar. The interior is layered with ceramics,

Al-Aqsa Mosque. Al-Aqsa has undergone many changes since its original construction. When the Crusaders captured Jerusalem in the 11th century al-Aqsa became the headquarters of the Templars. The mosque's design pales in comparison to the Dome of the Rock. It is off-limits to non–Muslim visitors.

Church of the Holy Sepulchre

Christian Quarter

The Christian Quarter is situated in the northwestern corner of the Old City. The quarter contains the Church of the Holy Sepulchre, one of Christianity's holiest places. It is the place where the Christian Bible says Jesus was killed and buried; every Christian group has historically sought to control this church. None of the communities controls it entirely. In order to avoid taking sides among the Christians, in 1192 the Ottoman rulers assigned responsibility for it to two neighboring Muslim families. The Joudeh were entrusted with the key, and the Nuseibeh were given the task of tending to the door. This arrangement continues today. Twice each day a Joudeh family member brings the key to the door, which is locked and unlocked by a Nuseibeh. On Sundays the bells of St. Ann's Church, another of many Jerusalem churches, can be heard throughout the Old City.

Other Things to See in the Christian Quarter

Lutheran Church of the Redeemer. This church was built by Kaiser Wilhelm II and completed in 1898. The church is most admired by tourists for its bell tower. At the top of its 177 steps visitors are rewarded with great views over the Old City.

Christian Quarter Road. Along with David Street, this *shuk* (outdoor market) is the quarter's main shopping thoroughfare. As with most shopping areas in the Christian Quarter, it specializes in religious items as well as handicrafts.

A Walk on the Roofs. It is possible to walk above the central *shuk* along the rooftops of the city. Visitors can climb up to the rooftops via two small staircases. The rooftops offer great views of the streets below. You can see the Church of the Holy Sepulcre and the Dome of the Rock as well.

The Shuk

Jerusalem rooftops

Jewish Quarter

The Jewish Quarter is the part of the Old City directly west of the ancient Temple Mount, where the great Temple once stood. Hence "the wall," the כֹּתֶל *Kotel*, is often called the Western Wall. By the time of King Hezekiah in 700 B.C.E., the eastern part of what is today the Jewish Quarter had been added to the city. During the Roman period the Jewish population revolted several times against their tyrannical rulers. The most famous of these revolts was the Bar Kokhba Revolt in 132 C.E.

After the fall of the Roman Empire in the fifth century, the Byzantine Christians controlled Jerusalem and forbade Jews to live in Jerusalem altogether. When the Muslim invasions began in the seventh century, Jewish communities moved into Jerusalem once again, thanks to more tolerant Muslim rule. In 1099, when the European Crusaders ransacked the ancient city, they celebrated their triumph by massacring most of the city's Jewish population as well as thousands of Muslims and local Christians.

In 1267, after the Crusaders were driven from Jerusalem, a small Jewish community reestablished itself in the ruins of what is now the Jewish Quarter. This area has been the center of the Jewish community in the Old City ever since. In 1948 its population of about two thousand Jews was forced to leave. The quarter had been completely sacked, with ancient synagogues destroyed. The quarter remained under Jordanian control

Paper Prayer

When you go to the Western Wall you will see hundreds of slips of paper stuffed into cracks. These are the prayers and wishes that people leave in a place they believe is a little closer to God. Use this slip of paper to write a prayer or wish you would like to leave at the Western Wall.

_____

_____

_____

_____

_____

_____

_____

_____

_____

_____

_____

_____

_____

_____

_____

_____

_____

_____

_____

until its capture by Israeli paratroopers in the Six-Day War in 1967. The Old City of Jerusalem is once again overseen by Jews in their sovereign state.

Today the Jewish Quarter thrives, with many yeshivot, bookstores, museums, and kosher restaurants lining its cobblestone streets.

Before being rebuilt the quarter was carefully excavated under the supervision of Hebrew University archaeologist Nahman Avigad. The archaeological remains, on display in a series of museums and outdoor parks that tourists descend two or three stories beneath the level of the current city to visit.

Things to See in the Jewish Quarter

The Western Wall. Known in Hebrew as הַכֹּתֶל הַמַּעֲרָבִי *Ha-Kotel Ha-Ma'aravi*, it dates back over two thousand years and marks the western edge of the Temple Mount. It is the only surviving remnant of the Temple Mount. As part of the retaining wall, it was built by Herod the Great during his expansion of the Temple in 20 B.C.E. The wall became the Jews' chief place of pilgrimage during the Ottoman Period; pilgrims lamented the destruction of the Temple at the hands of the Romans in 70 C.E. The plaza in front of the Wall is divided by a fence, with a large area for men on the left and a smaller area for women on the right. All are allowed to approach the wall as long as their heads are

Live Kotel Cam http://english.thekotel.org/cameras.asp

85

The Cardo

covered, they behave with decorum, and they are dressed appropriately. The wall acts as an outdoor synagogue, with written prayers inserted into the crevices between the large stones.

The Cardo. Coming from the same root as cardiac, heart, the Cardo once ran nearly the entire length of the Old City from north to south. The Cardo is an excavated and partially reconstructed section of the Jerusalem's main thoroughfare from the Roman and Byzantine eras. Visitors can get a good idea of how the whole once looked by descending to the 650-foot section alongside the Jewish Quarter. The central roadway was

41 feet wide and lined with shops. The pillars from that time still stand. Today in part the Cardo contains an exclusive covered shopping area.

Hurva Square. In a maze of narrow and winding streets Hurva Square is the heart and social center of the Jewish Quarter. Its open areas offer cafés, souvenir shops, and snack bars with outdoor seating. On the west side of the square are the ruins of the Hurva Synagogue (Hurva means "ruins"). Burned down by its creditors in the 18th century, the synagogue was rebuilt in 1864 only to be destroyed during the fighting that took place in 1948 between the Arab and Jewish armies. Today it's being rebuilt.

The Broad Wall. Following the 1967 occupation a vast reconstruction program in the Jewish Quarter resulted in many important archaeological finds. One of

Mount of Olives

the most significant was the unearthing of the foundations of a massive wall. These fortifications, measuring 22 feet thick and 215 feet long, may have been part of the fortifications built by King Hezekiah in the 8th century B.C.E.

Wohl Archaeological Museum. Ten to twenty-two feet below street level, this museum offers a vivid excavation showing daily life during the Herodian era two

thousand years ago, before the Romans rampaged and burned the wealthy Upper City in 69 C.E.

A Few Other Sites Near the Old City

Mount of Olives. The Mount of Olives הַר הַזֵּיתִים *Har ha-Zeitim* is a mountain ridge to the east of Jerusalem. It is named for the olive trees that cover its sides. In Hebrew, the word for olive is זַיִת *zayit*. In the Book of Zechariah the Mount of Olives is identified as the place from which God will begin to redeem the dead at the end of days. For this reason Jews have always sought to be buried there. From Biblical times to the present day the mountain has been used as a cemetery for the Jews of Jerusalem.

Warren's Shaft. This tunnel is located about 330 feet from the City of David excavations. Named after Charles Warren, its 19th-century discoverer, the sloping tunnel leads to a pool fed by the Gihon Spring. The system was built by the Jebusites to ensure a

City of David

Hezekiah's Tunnel

water supply during sieges. In the 10th century B.C.E. a tunnel was dug to take water from the Gihon Spring to the fields of the Kidron Valley. King Hezekiah built a new tunnel to bring the spring water right into the city. Hezekiah's Tunnel ran 1,750 feet from the spring to the Pool of Siloam in the south end of the city. Visitors can wade through the tunnel in thigh-deep water.

City of David. These ruins are the oldest part of Jerusalem, with remains of buildings up to the city's capture by the Babylonians in 586 B.C.E. The ruins include 13th century B.C.E. walls along with fortifications and fragments of a palace attributed to David, the second king of Israel. The site is located south of the Temple Mount. A small section of the excavation is open to the public, showing the house of Ahiel.

Getting Married in Jerusalem

The heart of a Jewish wedding is a series of seven blessings called the *Sheva Brakhot*. These are said at the wedding, during *Birkat ha-Mazon* at the wedding feast, and at every meal the couple attends for the next seven days. Below is the text of the seventh of these blessings.

Blessed are You, Eternal our God, Ruler of the Cosmos, Who has created joy and gladness, bridegroom and bride, happiness and celebration, pleasure and delight, love, human connection, peace and fellowship. Soon may there be heard in the cities of Judah, and in the streets of Jerusalem, the voice of joy and gladness, the voice of the groom and the voice of the bride, the happy voice of grooms from their wedding canopies, and of youths from their feasts of song. Blessed are You, Eternal, Who makes groom to rejoice with the bride.

1. What is the big idea of this blessing?
2. According to everything you have learned in this lesson about Jerusalem, why was it mentioned in this blessing?
3. Why do you think Jerusalem is part of every Jewish wedding? (Breaking the glass at the wedding also has a connection to Jerusalem.)

The Galilee

הַגָּלִיל

One reason that Israel has been historically important is that it is crossed by the only two ways to get from Egypt to Babylonia. The Nile Valley and the Tigris and Euphrates Valley were both places where major civilizations and powerful nations grew. It was always going to be the case that these two civilizations would want to trade with each other—and on ocasion would want to fight each other. There were only two roads. One was called the King's Highway; it went behind the Dead Sea and followed the Jordan Valley up to Damascus and then went north. The other was called the Way of the Sea. It followed the Coast of the Mediterranean Sea up to Dor, turned inland past the fortress city of Megiddo, headed through the Jezreel Valley, past the fortress city of Hazor, and joined the King's Highway in Damascus. This second path goes through the Galilee.

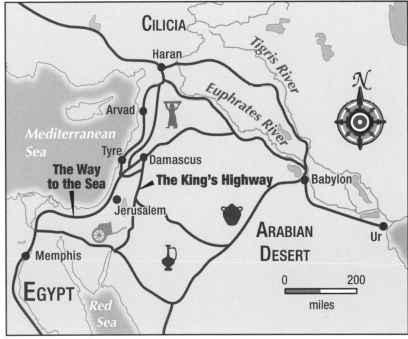

Megiddo

Megiddo is the name of a hill in the north of Israel. It is named after an ancient city-state and located near a modern settlement that bears the same name. According to some Christian sources, this is the site where, at the end of days, the final battle between the forces of light (led by Jesus) will fight the forces of evil (led by Satan). In other words, it is the venue of Armeggedon. There are some parallel Jewish legends. In ancient times Megiddo was an important site because it was the intersection point of the trade routes between Egypt and Assyria.

Megiddo is a *tel*. A *tel* is a hill or mound made up of a destroyed city built over a destroyed city. Megiddo is made of twenty-six such layers of the ruins of ancient cities in a strategic location at the head of a pass through the Carmel Ridge that overlooks the Valley of Jezreel. Megiddo was a site of great importance in the ancient world, as it guarded the western branch of a narrow pass and an ancient trade route that connected the lands of Egypt and Assyria. Because of its strategic location at the crossroads of several major routes, Megiddo witnessed several major battles throughout history. Three of the more famous battles include:

- Battle of Megiddo (15th century B.C.E.): fought between the armies of the Egyptian Pharoah Tutmose III and the rulers of Megiddo and Kadesh. This is the first documented battle in recorded history.

- Battle of Megiddo (609 B.C.E.): fought between Egypt and the Kingdom of Judah; King Josiah fell.

- Battle of Megiddo (1918): fought during World War I between Allied troops, led by General Edmund Allenby, and the defending Ottoman army.

Megiddo has been excavated three times.

The Galilee includes more than one-third of present-day Israel. It is mostly rocky terrain with some very fertile valleys. There are several high mountains, such as Mount Tavor and Mount Merom. The relatively low temperatures and the large amounts of rainfall make the Galilee a center of flora and wildlife; many birds pass by every year in their migration. The streams and waterfalls, along with vast fields and colorful wildflowers, make it a popular tourist attraction. The Galilee is a place to do a lot of hiking, camping, and picnicking.

The Galilee

The Kinneret (Sea of Galilee)

History of the Galilee

In the Bible, the Galilee is where the Northern Tribes settled. These included Asher, Dan, Naphtali, Zebulun, Issachar and Ephraim. When Solomon's son Rehoboam took over, Israel split into two kingdoms. In the north was Israel; in the south was Judah. Israel basically filled the Galilee.

During the Hasmonean period, with the revolt of the Maccabees and the decline of the Seleucid Empire (the Greeks), the region was conquered by the newly independent state of Judeah.

The Galilee was the home of Jesus during at least thirty years of his life. The first three Gospels of the Christian Scriptures are mainly an account of Jesus' life in the Galilee.

The Arab caliphate took control of the region in 638 C.E. The Shia Fatimids conquered the region in the 900s, and a breakaway sect formed the Druze religion. During the Crusades the Galilee was one of the most important Crusader districts. It was in the Galilee, at the Horns of Hattin in 1187 C.E. that Saladin defeated the Crusaders.

In the early twentieth century the Galilee was inhabited by Arabs, Druze, and Jews. The Jewish population increased significantly through Zionist immigration. A lot of it had to do with the creation of kibbutzim. After the War of Independence in 1949 the entire Galilee came under Israel's control. A large portion of the Arab population fled, leaving entire villages empty; however, more Arabs

Samir al-Atresh

I am Samir al-Atresh. My older sister is Fatimah. We are Druze and we live in a Druze village at the foot of Mount Hermon.

Nature is my favorite thing. I love hiking and exploring in the hills. I have a good time taking care of the goats and hens on our farm. I even like working in our garden, but not as much as I like just roaming on my own.

We Druze have a very secret religion so I can't tell you very much about it. I can tell you that our village has religious meetings on Thursday night. I go to a Druze school with other Druze children from villages all over our area. It is too far to walk. We take a bus there.

When I grow up I am going to join the Israeli army like every other member of my community. While we speak a kind of Arabic, we are not Muslims or Christians, and are welcome to serve our country, Israel.

remained in the Galilee than in most parts of Israel.

Modern Galilee

Today the Galilee is one of the few regions in Israel to have a large Arab population after the founding of the State in 1948, with a particularly large Druze population. The population of the Galilee is 44.3% Jewish and 52.5% Arab (including Druze and Bedouins).

Because of its hilly terrain, the Galilee is dotted mostly with settlements that are small villages connected by relatively few roads. The main economic activities in the area are agriculture and tourism. Industrial parks are being developed, bringing further employment opportunities to a local population that includes many recent immigrants.

The Galilee is a popular destination for vacationing Israelis from other parts of the country who enjoy its scenery, recreation and food. Many kibbutzim and moshavim operate guest houses.

Kibbutz

In the Galilee we are going to visit two different kibbutzim. One is Degania Alef, the oldest kibbutz in Israel. And the second, Kibbutz Lavi, is an kibbutz that earns a lot of its money through manufacturing synagogue furniture.

The kibbutz (communal settlement) is a society dedicated to mutual aid, social justice, and an economic system based on the principles of joint ownership. On a kibbutz everything is shared, everyone works and everyone gets what he or she needs.

Today some 270 kibbutzim with memberships ranging from 40 to more than 1,000 are scattered throughout the country. Most of them have between 300 and 400 adult members and a population of 500–600. The number of people living in kibbutzim totals approximately 130,000, about 2.5 percent of the country's population.

The kibbutz functions as a true democracy. Everyone votes. Members formulate policy, elect officers, authorize the kibbutz budget, and approve new members. When members of the kibbutz meet to make decisions, it is a chance for everyone to express his or her opinion.

Making the Desert Bloom

For the founders, the original חֲלוּצִים halutzim (pioneers) tilling the soil of their ancient homeland and transforming city dwellers into farmers was an ideology, not just a way to earn a livelihood. Kibbutzniks made barren lands bloom with field crops, orchards, poultry, dairy, and fish farming. Today organic agriculture is becoming one of the mainstays of their economy.

Through a combination of hard work and advanced farming methods kibbutzim achieved remarkable results. While most of them are still in agriculture, today

Meet the B'nai Sakhnin Football Club

Sakhnin

B'nai Sakhnin is an Israeli football club based at the Doha Stadium in the Arab village of Sakhnin.

They won the Israeli State Cup in 2004. They qualified to play in the UEFA Cup (European Cup 3)—the first time an Arab team from Israel ever got that far. "It's important for me and for all the Arabs in Israel and all the people who believe in peace and co-existence," said Shuwan Abbas, the team captain. "I think it's very important for the whole country to know how to practice co-existence."

"Sakhnin is a symbol for all the Arab minority inside Israel," says one fan. "It has 1.25 million people cheering for it. If the team wins, it's as if all the Arabs in this country win."

Israeli billionaire Arcadi Gaydamak donated $400,000 in the hope of promoting peace and harmony among the citizens of Israel. The gift allowed the team to return to their rebuilt home stadium, largely financed by the Emir of Qatar.

During the 2005-06 season the club signed a shirt sponsorship deal with Israeli mobile phone company Cellcom. The fan base of B'nai Sakhnin is small in comparison to other Israeli clubs. The majority of fans of B'nai Sakhnin are Arab Israelis, but the club also has many Jewish Israeli fans from the neighboring kibbutzim.

virtually all kibbutzim have also expanded into various kinds of industry.

The Work Ethic

Work is a major kibbutz value. Kibbutzniks believe that the dignity of labor elevates the most menial job. Members are assigned to positions for varying lengths of time, while routine functions such as kitchen and dining hall duty are performed on a rotation basis.

Even from the very beginning of the kibbutz movement women are equal participants in the labor force, with jobs in all parts of the kibbutz open to them. Older members receive work assignments that fit with their health and strength.

Raising Children

Unlike the early days of the kibbutz, all the children used to livea nd sleep togther in children's houses. Today many sleep at their parents' homes. However, most of their waking hours are still spent with their peers in houses set up specifically for each age group. The family unit is gaining more importance in the the kibbutz community.

From kindergarten, the educational system emphasizes cooperation in daily life, and from the early school grades, youngsters are assigned duties and make decisions with regard to their peer group. Young children perform regular age-appropriate tasks, older children assume certain jobs in the kibbutz, and at high school level they devote one full day each week to work in a branch of the kibbutz economy. Elementary schools are usually on the kibbutz premises, while older children attend a regional kibbutz high school serving several area kibbutzim. Some 40 percent of all kibbutz children return to settle on their kibbutz after army service. The majority of kibbutz members today grew up in the kibbutz and decided to build their life there.

Celebrating Shavuot on Kibbutz

Degania Alef

A child passes by on the road leading to the main entrance of the Kibbutz Degania Alef.

Degania (from דָּגָן *dagan*, meaning grain), located south of Lake Kinneret, was established in 1909 on land acquired by the Jewish National Fund. The founders were young Jewish pioneers, mainly from Eastern Europe, who came not only to reclaim the soil of their ancient homeland, but also to forge a new way of life. They were inexperienced with physical labor and had a lack of agricultural know-how while working with desolate land neglected for centuries. There was scarcity of water and a shortage of funds. Overcoming many hardships, they succeeded in developing thriving communities that played a dominant role in the establishment of the State of Israel.

Degania Alef has been home to many famous Israelis. The poet Rachel, the "prophet of labor" A.D. Gordon, Joseph Trumpledor, and the first lady of Israeli song, Naomi Shemer, are all buried at Degania Alef. Moshe Dayan, a famous military leader, was the second child born at Degania Alef.

Degania Alef is different from most kibbutzim in that children always slept in their parents' quarters.

In 2007 Degania Alef announced that it was making a change. Instead of assigned jobs and equal pay, people are able to seek their jobs, earn their salaries, and own their homes.

Degania Alef

Degania Diary

This is what the pioneers who founded Degania Alef wrote:

"On the 28th of October 1910, there arrived at Umm Juni, ten men and two women. We came to establish an independent settlement of Hebrew laborers, on national land, a collective settlement with neither exploiters nor exploited—a commune."

From the archives of Degania Alef

1. What did these _halutzim_ mean when they said "We came to establish an independent settlement of Hebrew laborers, on national land"?

2. What did these _halutzim_ mean by "a collective settlement with neither exploiters nor exploited—a commune"?

Reconstruction of the "Wall and Tower" defense system used at early kibbutzim.

Young workers in the kibbutz date grove

Rachel

Rachel (1890–1931) was born Rachel Bluwstein in Russia the eleventh child of Isser-Leib and Sophia Bluwstein and granddaughter of the rabbi of Kiev. At fifteen she started to write poetry, and at seventeen she studied painting. Rachel moved to the Land of Israel at nineteen and settled with her sister in a community on the shore of the Kinneret, Israel's largest freshwater lake. As a pioneer poet she wrote poetry on love, loss, longing for home, the pain she suffered from being unable to have children, and the pastoral beauty and miracles of the land of Israel. She used many biblical themes and stories in her poems. Many of her poems were set to music during her lifetime and afterward. She is buried on the shores of the Kinneret at Kibbutz Degania Alef, as she requested in her poem *If Fate Decrees*. She died of tuberculosis at the age of forty-one.

When Naomi Shemer, a famous Israeli poet and folk musician (who wrote, among other songs, *Yerushalayim shel Zahav*), was near to death, she asked to be buried beside Rachel. "Rachel the poet" is the most famous Israeli poet to this day, and her collection of poetry remains one of the most popular publications in Israel.

1. Why do you think *Eretz Yisrael* meant so much to Rachel?
2. Why did Naomi Shemer want to be buried next to Rachel?

A Poem by Rachel

For My Country

I have not sung to you, my country,
And I have not glorified your name
With heroic deeds
Or the plunder of battles.
Only a tree—that my hands planted
On the quiet shores of the Jordan.
Only a path—that my feet have conquered
Through the fields.

Indeed, it is very poor—
I know this, mother.
Indeed, it is very poor—
This offering from your daughter.
Only the voice of joyous song
When the day's light arrives,
Only secret tears
For your poverty.

(translation by Joel Grishaver and Josh Mason-Barkin)

1. What does Rachel say she is doing for the Land of Israel?
2. Why is this a big contribution?
3. Why does Rachel cry for the Land of Israel?
4. What is she doing about it?

Woman harvesting dates on kibbutz

Kibbutz Lavi

Pundak Lavi, the Lion's Inn, is mentioned by name in the Talmud. The story is that some people found a block of cheese at the *pundak,* and the rabbis allowed them to eat it because the Jews there were pious and would never have cheese that wasn't kosher.

Kibbutz Lavi is a religious kibbutz. Lavi has a guest house and a factory that makes furniture for synagogues. Kibbutz Lavi was actually founded in 1949 by teenagers who had been passengers on the *Kindertransport* that helped children escape the Holocaust in Germany to go to England. The layout of the kibbutz reflects its values: The synagogue is in the center, surrounded by buildings for everyday life.

Across from the synagogue is a place of study and a library that contains, among other things, a memorial room with books on the life of each kibbutznik who has died.

Next to the dining room is the laundry; behind it is the *mikvah* (ritual bath). The plains below (past the cows) are where the battle of the Horn of Hattin took place and the Crusaders lost the kingdom of Jerusalem. To the right is Tiberias; to the left, on the Kinneret, stands the city of Zippori.

This being a religious kibbutz, the cows were a source of talmudic debate: What to do with them on Shabbat? It is a mitzvah to milk cows on Shabbat because they would be in pain if you didn't. The verdict of the rabbis: Don't buy cows. But kibbutzniks came up with their own solution. Making use of alternative milking methods, the dairy is hooked up to switches that work on air pressure—thus avoiding electricity—to turn on the milking machines automatically on Shabbat.

Kibbutz Lavi boasts the world's largest synagogue furniture factory. Over 2,000 synagogues have furniture from Kibbutz Lavi.

Kibbutz Meeting

You are a member of a new kibbutz. It is time for a big meeting that will decide the child-raising philosophy.

Divide your class in half. Have each half represent one of the two positions. Hold the kibbutz meeting and make a decision.

Children's Houses: Traditionally, kibbutzim had children of the same age live together in a house. They would spend the late afternoon and dinner with their parents and then return to sleep with their hevrah (group). The idea was that learning to be part of a community was as important as being part of a family.

Children Live at Home: Today most kibbutzim have children sleep at home. They still spend most of the day with their hevrah. The new popular opinion is that children need a stronger balance of family and community.

Write an argument for your side.

_____

_____

_____

_____

_____

The Last Kibbutz—Israel/Palestine (http://tiny.cc/qth17)

Golan

The Golan Heights (*Ramat ha-Golan*) is a plateau on the border of Israel, Lebanon, Jordan, and Syria. Captured by Israel from Syria in the 1967 War, the Golan Heights is the northernmost region of the country and perhaps the most beautiful. Its volcanic mountains and valleys create excellent conditions for growing grapes. Many of Israel's vineyards are located here.

Fifty percent of Israel's water supply comes from the Golan, which guarantees that the water source, the Kinneret, is accessed exclusively by Israel.

It also has Israel's only ski resort, at Mount Hermon. Cattle graze in the upland plateau. The area is also popular for hiking. In 2005 the Golan Heights had a population of approximately 38,900, including approximately 19,300 Druze, 16,500 Jews, and 2,100 Muslims.

CHALLENGE FOR ISRAEL

WATER MANAGEMENT

Water is Israel's most important national resource. When you live in a really dry country it is important that you have clean water to drink and to water crops. Israel has suffered a serious water shortage. The situation has developed into a major crisis.

The causes of this crisis are both natural and human-made. Israel has suffered from several consecutive years of drought. Add to this an increase in demand for water for domestic use caused by population growth and the rising standard of living. Farms have suffered most. Water for farming has been reduced drastically.

After drawing on nearly all of its available water resources and promoting vigorous conservation programs, Israel has made it a national mission to stretch existing sources. Water conservation is the most reliable and least expensive way to stretch the country's water resources. The use of low-volume irrigation systems such as drip agriculture and micro-sprinklers has increased the average efficiency to 90%.

Soon the Point of No Return (http://tiny.cc/artc0)

Map of the Galilee

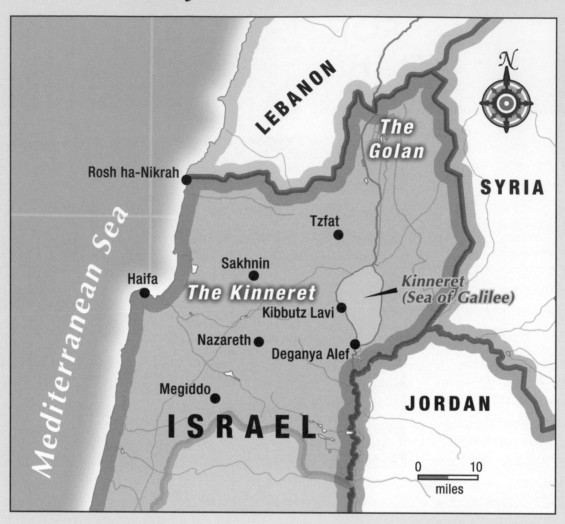

Fill in the missing places.

1. In English it is called the Sea of Galilee _____

2. Kibbutz that makes synagogue furniture_____

3. Area with Israel's only ski resort _____

4. First kibbutz _____

5. Archaeological site with 26 layers of destroyed cities _____

6. Arab town with winning soccer team _____

Three Other Places to Visit in the Galilee

Tiberias is a city that has been a tourist

destination for more than two thousand years. It is located on the western shore of the Kinneret and offers some nice lake side hotels for tourists. Tiberias' hot springs make it an especially popular winter resort.

Tiberias was a center of Jewish learning from its founding in 19 C.E. until the Middle Ages. The city was founded by Herod Antipas. Herod named the city for the emperor Tiberius. After the Roman destruction of the Temple in Jerusalem in 70 C.E. Jewish scholars began to settle in Tiberias. The highest rabbinical court, the Sanhedrin, met in Tiberias. The Jerusalem Talmud, a body of commentaries on Jewish civil and religious law, was compiled primarily in Tiberias between the third and fifth centuries C.E. The tomb of Maimonides is located in Tiberias.

Tiberias is a great place to take a cruise on the Kinneret and to eat out on the lake shore. (Try a restaurant called Decks.)

Katzrin is the administrative center and

largest town in the Golan Heights. The town has great views of the surrounding landscapes.

Katzrin is a major center of tourism in the Golan Heights due to its historical sites. One of these is the ancient Talmudic village of Kisrin (the source of the name Katzrin), which was destroyed in the eighth century by an earthquake. The village has archaeological remains of a synagogue, partially reconstructed, and foundations of ancient houses. The Museum of Golan Antiquities displays the archaeological finds uncovered in the Golan. Katzrin is home to a kosher winery and a mineral water plant.

The Banyas Nature Reserve, also

called Nahal Hermon Reserve, encompasses the upper Nahal Hermon, the Banyas waterfall, and a number of archaeological sites, including remains of a Greek temple dedicated to the goat-footed god Pan. The trails in the reserve pass along bubbling springs, brooks, and waterfalls in the midst of thick riverbank vegetation. The reserve provides a great refuge from the sun even in summer.

The Negev

הַנֶּגֶב

A As Israel's population grows, its central region is running out of space. The Negev Desert is a massive land area waiting to be developed. It is 60% of Israel's land mass with only 8% of Israel's population. The Jewish National Fund has a goal to bring 250,000 new residents to the Negev in the next five years. Ben-Gurion, the first Prime Minister of Israel, who moved to Kibbutz Sde Boker in the Negev, said, "The Negev will be the test of the creative ability and pioneering spirit of Israel."

The Negev is the desert region of southern Israel. The origin of the word נֶגֶב *Negev* is from the Hebrew root that means dry. In the Bible the word נֶגֶב is also used for the direction south.

The Negev is a rocky desert. It is a mixture of brown, rocky, dusty mountains, wadis (dry riverbeds that bloom briefly after rain), and deep craters. The area actually was once the floor of a primordial sea. A sprinkling of marine snail shells still covers the earth there.

History of the Negev

We know about nomads who wandered the Negev seven thousand years ago. The first settlements were established 2000 B.C.E. Egypt is credited with beginning copper mining and smelting in both the Negev and Sinai around 1300 B.C.E. Small settlements of Jews existed between 1020 and 928 B.C.E.

The fourth century B.C.E. saw the arrival of the Nabataeans, who developed desert irrigation systems that supported at least five new urban centers. The Nabataeans controlled the trade and spice route between their capital, Petra (where one of the Indiana Jones movies was shot), and the seaports of Gaza.

The Roman empire took over their lands in 106 C.E. Byzantine rule in the fourth century C.E. introduced Christianity to the population. Agricultural-based cities were established, and the population grew. The arrival of Muslim forces in the seventh century was accepted with relative ease by the population due

Oasis in the Desert
(http://tiny.cc/vniyyj)

Nabataeans

Although not as dry as it is today, the area occupied by the Nabataeans was still a desert and required special systems for agriculture. One of their systems was to contour an area of land into a shallow funnel and to plant a single fruit tree in the middle. Before the rainy season, which could easily consist of only a one or two rains a year, the area around the tree was broken up. When the rain came, all the water that collected in the funnel would flow down toward the fruit tree and sink into the ground. The ground, which was largely loose, would seal up and retain the water when it got wet.

In the mid-1950s a team headed by M. Evenari set up a research station near Avdat. He focused on the relevance of runoff rainwater management and the ancient agricultural features as terraced wadis and channels. Evenari showed that the runoff rainwater collection systems concentrated water from an area five times larger than the area in which the water actually drained.

Today, many of the kibbutzim in the Negev use Nabataean water technology to grow crops in the desert.

to their shared Arab background, and Islam was easily accepted, too.

Nomadic tribes ruled the Negev independently and without interference until the modern era.

Avdat, a Nabataean settlement

The Negev Today

Today the Negev is home to some 379,000 Jews and 175,000 Bedouins. The region's largest city and administrative capital is Beersheva (population around 200,000). At its southern end is the the resort city of Eilat. The desert is home to Ben-Gurion University, which includes the Jacob Blaustein Institutes for Desert Research and the Albert Katze International School for Desert Studies, both located at Midreshet Ben-Gurion next to Sde Boker.

A Bedouin

Bedouins

The Negev Bedouins are nomadic tribes who have inhabited the desert for more than seven thousand years. Although unchanged throughout history, the tribal culture and way of life has altered recently. The Bedouins of the Negev survive on raising sheep and goats. Scarcity of water and of pastoral land requires them to move constantly. The Bedouins have established very few permanent settlements.

Bedouins are defined as nomad Arabs who live by rearing livestock in the deserts of southern Israel. The Negev Bedouin community consists of numerous indigenous tribes who used to be nomadic or semi-nomadic.

Between 1940 and 1966 the Bedouins were placed under military administration by Israel. As Jewish immigration increased, unemployment levels in the Bedouin population reached record highs. During this period Israel also enforced mandatory schooling for Bedouin children. As a result there was a general rise in literacy levels. The Bedouins also benefited from the introduction of modern techniques of health care.

Today around half the population lives in seven towns built for them by the Israeli government between 1979 and 1982. The largest Bedouin locality in Israel is the city of Rahat.

Beersheva

Beersheva is often referred to as the Capital of the Negev. In 2005, when the population reached 185,000, it became the sixth-largest city in Israel. בְּאֵר *Be'er* is a Hebrew word for "well." שֶׁבַע *Sheva* can mean either "oath" or "seven." That makes Beersheva the oath of Abraham and Abimelech (well of the oath) or the seven wells dug by Isaac (seven wells).

Bedouin Market

The Egyptian army was stationed in Beersheva in May 1948, during the War of Independence. Positive that Beersheva was important for the security of the Jewish state, Prime Minister David Ben-Gurion gave the green light for Operation Yoav during the War of Independence. On October 21, 1948, at four in the morning, the 82nd Battalion advanced from the Mishmar ha-Negev junction. By 9:45 the Egyptian forces were surrounded, and Beersheva was in Israeli hands.

Ben Gurion University, Beersheva

In the 1990s the population and size of Beersheva was substantially increased by a large influx of Russian and Ethiopian immigrants. In 1982 Israel evacuated by air a large portion of the Jewish community of Ethiopia. Many of them were settled in Beersheva. There are now approximately ten thousand Ethiopian Israelis living in Beersheva. To remind the members of the villages they left behind, the roof of the community center is a conic shape, much like their old homes.

The most popular sport in Beersheva is soccer, led by Hapoel Beersheva. Beersheva is also Israel's leading chess center. The local chess club has won many cups and national championships. It represented Israel in the European Cup and hosted the world team championship in 2005. Beersheva has a higher percentage of grand masters per capita than any other city in the world. Eight grand masters live in Beersheva.

Ilan Ramon

Crew of space shuttle *Columbia*

Ilan Ramon

Ilan Ramon (1954–2003) was a combat pilot in the Israeli Air Force and later the first Israeli astronaut. Ramon was the payload specialist on the fatal mission of space shuttle *Columbia*. Ramon was a recipient of the Congressional Space Medal of Honor. He was born in Ramat Gan and grew up in Beersheva. His mother and grandmother survived Auschwitz.

Even though Ramon was a secular Jew, he sought to observe Jewish traditions while in orbit. He said, "I feel I am representing all Jews and all Israelis." He was the first space flight participant to request kosher food.

Aboard the shuttle Ramon carried a pencil sketch, "Moon Landscape," drawn by fourteen-year-old Petr Ginz, who died in Auschwitz. Ramon also took a copy of the Torah given to him by Israeli president Moshe Katsav. Ramon asked the 1939 Club, a Holocaust survivor organization, for a symbol of the Holocaust to take with him. A barbed-wire mezuzah by San Francisco artist Aimee Golant was selected. Ramon also took with him a dollar from Rabbi Menachem M. Schneerson, the Lubavitcher Rebbe.

On February 1, 2003, when Columbia was on its way home, a malfunction caused the shuttle to explode over Texas. The whole crew died, including Israel's first astronaut, Ilan Ramon.

The Negev Foundation

Sabra

It is hard to grow things in the desert. Working to grow things in the desert is a major part of the growth of the Negev. It takes new ways of thinking about water and other natural resources to make this happen, The Negev Foundation works on finding plants that can grow with little water and finding new ways of using water. Growing with brackish water (part salt water, part fresh) and using grey water (water reused that is not completely pure) are some of the things they have pioneered.

When the Ramat Negev Desert AgroResearch Center was first conceived, it was located close to water sources and existing roads. Large quantities of sand were trucked in at considerable expense. They have had huge success with sand as a soil substitute for plant cultivation.

Aquaculture is growing fish in pools. It is a new field in Israel due to economic need and the abundant supply of brackish waters. Cultivated fish account for 20% of the total world fish consumption today. In responding to this trend, Israeli scientists are perfecting the growth of new fish varieties.

All this is part of the greening of the Negev.

Kibbutz Lotan

Captain Compost

An old Zionist song goes, "We came to the land to build it and to be built by it." In many ways that is the story of Kibbutz Lotan. The kibbutz is looking to "greenly" make the desert green.

The Lotan Park is part of the Tzell ha-Tamar Non-Profit Association. It is an experiential ecological education center that focuses on recycling, organic gardening, and alternative building as modern Jewish *mitzvot* based on traditional Jewish texts and sources.

Highlights at the Center include Noah's Ark, a playground built of used tires, garbage, and local earth; Captain Compost and His Compost

Israeli, Jordanian, and Palestinian Youths Become "Eco-builders" at Kibbutz Lotan (http://tiny.cc/oetku)

Educational Corner, with splendid organic vegetable gardens and orchards; The Living Dome, a geodesic dome covered in vines, where guests are served organic herbal tea cooked in a solar oven; and the Bird watching Park, a partnership with the Jewish National Fund, The Society for the Protection of Nature in Israel, and Birding International. The park will be irrigated by recycled wastewater from the kibbutz dairy, processed biologically by constructed wetlands.

The community also features green buildings "mostly of mud and straw with abundant use of trash" bottles, cans, and tires as building materials. There is graywater recycling and permaculture gardening (gardening that preserves rather than diminishes the environment). The kibbutz has only four cars for one hundred people! Lotan makes its living largely off its date plantation and dairy operation.

Rivkah Alemayehu

My name is Rivkah, a good Hebrew name, even though my family comes from Ethiopia. Part of my family moved in 1984 during Operation Moses, the rest came in 1991 during Operation Solomon. These two "operations" were airlifts bringing black Jews from Ethiopia to live in Israel.

In Ethiopia we were often called Falasha. That name was an insult. It means "exiles" or "strangers." We call ourselves "Beta Yisrael," the House of Israel. Some legends connect our origin to King Solomon and the Queen of Sheba. Others say the connection is Moses' wife from the Land of Cush (Ethiopia).

We have our own Ethiopian Jewish festival called Sigd. It comes on the 29th of the Hebrew month of Heshvan. The holiday symbolizes the handing down of the Torah. The word itself is Amharic (the language we speak) for bowing. It forms one of two Ethiopian Jewish terms for synagogue. During the celebration, members of the community fast, recite Psalms, and gather in Jerusalem where our Rabbis called Kessim read from the Orit, one of our holy books. The ritual is followed by the breaking of the fast, dancing, and partying.

I am all excited that a museum highlighting the culture and heritage of the Ethiopian Jewish community is to be built in Rehovot. I am really proud of my people and their tradition. One of my favorite things to do is cook Ethiopian Jewish dishes. The most popular traditional food in Ethiopia is 'injera', a type of spongy, thin bread made from 'tif' flour. 'Tif' is a small corn that grows in Ethiopia. Since the climate in Israel is not appropriate for growing 'tif', merchants bring 'tif' and sell it to the Ethiopian community in Israel. Injera is usually eaten with sauce and meat, vegetables and beans. The sauce is called 'waat' and is well flavored and very spicy. A traditional Ethiopian meal is eaten only with fingers. Silverware is not used.

Eilat

Eilat

Eilat is a tourist resort and port located on the Red Sea. It is Israel's southernmost city and part of the Negev Desert. Eilat is adjacent to the Egyptian village of Taba to the south and the Jordanian port city of Aqaba to the east. Eilat is named after the Eilat in the Bible. The city's beaches, nightlife, and desert landscapes make it a popular destination for domestic and international tourism.

The original settlement was probably at the northern tip of the Red Sea, now on the border with Jordan. It was a commercial port city and a copper-based economic center. Archaeological excavations uncovered impressive prehistoric tombs dating to the seventh millennium B.C.E., while nearby copper workings and mining operations at Timna Valley are

114

the oldest on earth. Ancient Egyptian records also record extensive mining operations.

Eilat is mentioned several times in the Bible. It was one of the stops that the Families of Israel made during the Exodus from Egypt. King David conquered Edom and took over Eilat as well. During the Roman period a road was built to link the area with the fabulous Nabataean city of Petra. The remains of a large copper smelting and trading community that flourished during the Ummayad Period (700 C.E.) were also found.

Aqua Park

Eilat offers many attractions and recreational
options within a 35-mile radius.

- Freefall parchuting.
- Camel tours.
- Coral Beach Nature Reserve, an
  underwater marine reserve of tropical
  marine flora and fauna.
- Coral World, an underwater observatory
  that allows visitors to view marine life
  in its own habitat. The park, located at
  the southern tip of Coral Beach, has
  aquariums, a museum, rides, as well as
  shark, turtle, and stingray tanks.
- Skin diving, snorkelling, and scuba diving
- Dolphin Reef, offering visitors an
  opportunity to swim and interact with
  dolphins.

- Hai-Bar Yotvata Nature Reserve, which reintroduces wild animals, including biblical species, that were extinct in this region and bolsters populations of endangered species from similar climates. The reserve has a visitors center, care and treatment enclosures, and a large open area where desert animals are acclimated before re-introduction into the wild.
- Kings City, a biblical theme park located in the hotel area next to the Stella Maris Lagoon.
- Ostrich farm.
- Bedouin hospitality.
- Marina with 250 yacht berths.
- Texas Ranch, inspired by an actual movie set washed away in a flood. This is a camel and horse ranch with organized riding excursions. Several movies have been filmed here.
- Bird watching. Eilat is located on the main migration route between Africa and Europe.
- Timna Valley Park, the oldest copper mine in the world.
- Egyptian Temple of Hathor and King Solomon's Pillars geologic formations.

Ben-Gurion

David Ben-Gurion is the Israeli George Washington. He was the founding father of Israel. He was the first signer of the declaration. In 1948 he became the first Prime Minister of the State of Israel, a position he held until 1963 (1954 and 1955 excepted). He was a central figure in the forming the Histadrut (the national labor union) and the Haganah (the Jewish defense organization before the new state was established). Ben-Gurion insisted that the newly declared state would have only one unified defense mechanism: the Israeli Defense Forces. He led the new state to victory in the the War of Independence, in which the Arab countries surrounding Israel waged war on Israel after the country declared independence. His main project as prime minister was the absorption of millions of Jewish immigrants who could finally be brought in without worrying about British quotas. Operation Magic Carpet brought thousands of Jews living in Arab lands to the newly established State of Israel. This helped to increase the number of Jews in Israel and liberate these Jews from second-class status and increasing persecution in Muslim countries.

The international airport in Tel Aviv bears his name, as does the Ben-Gurion University of the Negev. He chose to spend the last years of his life on Kibbutz Sde Boker, helping to settle the Negev.

1. Write a one sentence obituary of David Ben Gurion.
2. Why do you think he chose to spend his final years in the Negev?

The Magic of the Negev

Ben-Gurion wrote this about the Negev:

The desert gives us the best opportunity to begin again. This is a vital element of our renewal in Israel. For it is through mastering nature that people learn to control themselves. It is in this sense that I define our Redemption on this land. Israel must continue to cultivate its nationality. It must earn this, a right that can only be acquired in the desert.

When I looked out my window today and saw a tree standing before me, the sight awoke in me a greater sense of beauty and personal satisfaction than all the forests that I have crossed in Switzerland and Scandinavia. For we planted each tree in this place and watered them with the water we provided through much effort. Why does a mother love her children so? Because they are her creation. Why does the Jew feel an affinity with Israel? Because everything here must still be accomplished. It depends only on the individual Jew to participate in this privileged act of creation. The trees at Sde Boker speak to me differently than do the trees planted elsewhere. Not only because I participated in their planting and in their maintenance, but also because they are a person's gift to nature.

1. For Ben-Gurion, what makes a tree at Sde Boker different from other trees?

   _____

   _____

2. How does the desert give us the chance to start over? What is special about the desert?

   _____

   _____

Three Other Places to Visit in the Negev

Mitzpe Ramon is a Negev town. It is 2,400 feet up on the northern ridge of an enormous karst erosion cirque known as the Ramon Crater.

Mitzpe Ramon was originally founded in 1951 as a camp for workers building the road to Eilat. The town's first permanent residents, immigrants from North Africa and Romania, settled there in the 1960s. Mitzpe Ramon is a place for ecotourism: jeep trekking, repelling, climbing, and hiking.

Kibbutz Yotvata is along the Arava road in the southern Negev. Yotvata was established in 1957 as the first kibbutz in the southern Arava region. The ancient copper mines of Timna are located nearby. It is one of the most successful and stable kibbutzim because of its famed dairy business and its chain of vegetarian dairy restaurants.

In the early years the production line was limited to milk, *leben*, *eshel*, and sour cream. The entire factory was run by four members, giving it a family atmosphere. This tradition is one that has carried on through the years as the dairy has grown. Beginning in 1979 Yotvata Dairy expanded its market north of Beersheva and today its products can be found all over the country. The variety of products grew to include chocolate milk, flavored puddings, yogurt with fruit, and white cheeses ranging from cream cheese to low-fat cheese.

Yotvata Hai-Bar Nature Reserve is

stocked with acacia trees and includes a variety of desert habitats: an acacia forest, a salt marsh, and sand dunes.

The reserve has three parts: a three-acre penned-in open area where herds of herbivorous animals live in conditions similar to those in the wild; the Predators Center, where reptiles, small desert animals, and large predators are on display; and the Desert Night Life Exhibition Hall, where night and day are reversed so that visitors to the reserve can observe nocturnal animals during their active hours.

CHALLENGE FOR ISRAEL

LIVING WITH ONE'S NEIGHBORS

Lebanon, Syria, Jordan, Saudi Arabia, and Egypt all share borders with Israel. Historically these countries have been against Israel and the building of a Jewish State. There have been many wars between Israel and her Arab neighbors in the last sixty years.

Egypt and Jordan have signed peace treaties and normalized relations with Israel. But Lebanon, Syria, and Saudi Arabia still do not recognize the State of Israel. The Palestinians complicate these matters. Until Israel resolves that conflict, much of the tension with Arab nations is made worse by the Palestinian situation. Peace is very difficult to get to.

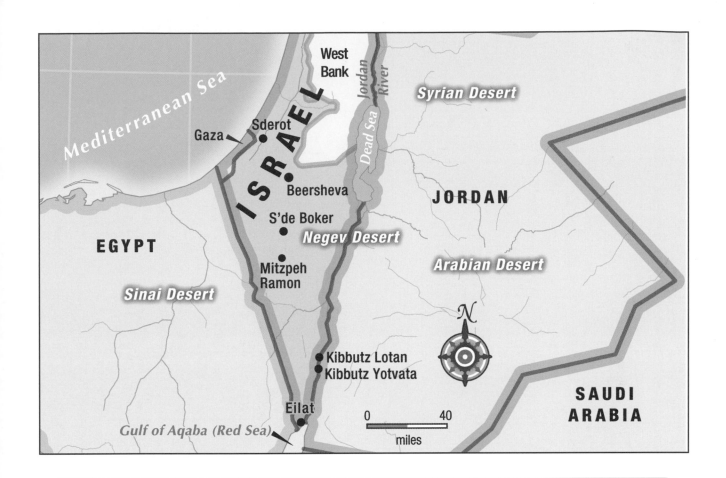

Greening the Negev

Imagine that you were building a new kibbutz in the Negev. One of your commitments is to make your kibbutz as ecologically friendly as you can. Hold a kibbutz meeting. Work out a list of the top five things you can do to make your kibbutz environmentally friendly.

1. _____

2. _____

3. _____

4. _____

5. _____

Drip irrigation

Tzfat

צְפַת

Tzfat is a small town located 3,000 feet above sea level in the mountains of the Upper Galilee. It is the highest city in Israel. According to the great mystics of the past, Tzfat is to play an important role in the final redemption. The *Meam Loez*, in the name of Rabbi Shimon bar Yo<u>h</u>ai, says that the Messiah will come from Tzfat on his way to Jerusalem. The Ari (Rabbi Isaac Luria) said that until the Third Temple is built, the *Shekhinah* (God's Presence) rests above Tzfat.

The History of Tzfat

According to legend, Tzfat is where Shem and Ever, son and grandson of Noah, established the yeshiva where Abraham, Isaac, and Jacob each studied for many years. More historical sources say that the town was founded in 70 c.e.. The earliest known Jewish settlement in Tzfat seems to have been in the time of the Second Temple, because it is mentioned both in the Talmud and in various prayers composed during the Talmudic period. In Crusader times (twelfth to thirteenth centuries) the town developed as "a fortress of very great strength between Akko and the Sea of Galilee." In 1266 it passed from the Crusaders to the Mamluks, who improved conditions for its citizens. Toward the end of the Mamluk rule the Jewish community was greatly strengthened by an influx of refugees from Spain. The Sefardi population increased after the conquest of Tzfat by the Ottoman Empire in 1516.

The city flourished in the sixteenth century, when many famous scholars and mystics moved there following the Spanish Expulsion. Tzfat was then the spiritual center of the Jewish world, the place where Kabbalah (Jewish mysticism) reached the peak of its influence.

Rabbi Isaac Luria (Ha-Ari ha-Kodesh), Rabbi Shlomo Alkabetz (the author of *Lekha Dodi*), Moses Cordovero (*The Remark*), and Rabbi Yosef Karo (the author of the *Shul<u>h</u>an Arukh*) were among those who made the city famous. It was here that the first printing press in the Middle East was set up by Eliezer Ashkenazi and his son, Isaac of Prague, publishing

Tzfat Israel Video Tour
(http://tiny.cc/67n2m)

in 1578 the first Hebrew book to be printed in Israel. This was a time when the town was a trade center. However, Tzfat suffered terribly during the following years. Earthquakes, plagues, and Arab attacks all led to an exodus. In modern times the liberation of Tzfat was one of the most dramatic episodes in the War of Independence.

Tzfat is one of Israel's four holy cities. Jerusalem, Hebron, and Tiberias are the others. The old part of town consists of narrow cobblestone alleys with artists' galleries, medieval synagogues, private homes, and small guest houses.

The Tzfat Artists' Colony

Artists were drawn to Tzfat and its mystical atmosphere long before the Artists' Colony was established. Mordechai Lavanon and Moshe Castel settled here in the 1930s. Mordechai Shemi arrived in 1947, followed by a wave of artists who settled here after the establishment of the State. Today the Artists' Quarter attracts thousands of tourists from all over the world who come to wander through the cobblestone alleys and to visit the artists in their studios and galleries.

When you wander the Artists' Colony, Jewish mysticism is never far away. Throughout the Artists' Quarter you will find a uniquely Jewish art form, microcalligraphy, in which images are made out of words (usually written small) from the Bible or other Jewish sources.

The most well-known art in Tzfat, other than candles, is microcalligraphy art. In these paintings, entire sections of the Bible are inscribed into watercolor paintings of biblical scenes as the lines of the pictures.

"I knew I desperately wanted one of these paintings showing the biblical scene of Jacob wrestling the Angel, but I didn't anticipate I would find one. I walked into one gallery and the artist/owner said, "I see your name tag. What is your Hebrew name?"

I told him, and he said, "I have a painting of your biblical namesake. Here, let me show you."

He pulled open a drawer and took out an amazing pience of art. "Look," he said, pointing to the top corner. "Your namesake, with his brothers."

But then I looked at the bottom, and there, in the lower right-hand corner, was a picture of Jacob wrestling the Angel.

And as I looked closely at the lines that made up Jacob I saw a very familiar part of the Torah.

The part I read sixteen years earlier. My *parashah*. My bar mitzvah Torah portion."

http://blunderingamerican.blogspot.com/ search?q=microcaligraphy

125

Book of Exodus; Parting of the Reed Sea. Ellen Miller Braun etched this intricate design on paper after doing a word count of the entire Book of Exodus. The word count prepared her for how tiny she would need to write to fit the Book of Exodus on this size paper. Once the design was etched and the letter size was determined, Ellen dipped her calligraphy pen in watercolor paints, and began writing each word from the Book of Exodus to create this masterful illustration of Parting of the Reed Sea. The entire process took 11 patience-filled months. (www.nishmati.co.il)

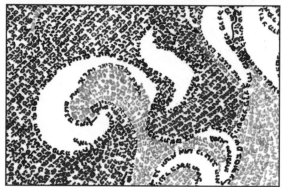

Micro Your Own Calligraphy

1. Pick a biblical text you want to illustrate.
   - Creation: Genesis 1.1—24
   - Jacob's Ladder: Genesis 28.10—22
   - Moses getting the Ten Commandments: Exodus 24.12—18
   - Moses looks at the land of Israel: Deuteronomy 34.1—5

2. Make a pencil outline of the artwork you want to create.

3. Either by following the pencil line or by filling it with the verses, make your own microcalligraphy creation.

The Kabbalah

We can't talk about Tzfat without talking about Kabbalah. Kabbalah wasn't started in Tzfat. Kabbalah is still evolving today. But Kabbalah came of age in Tzfat during the sixteenth century.

Kabbalah comes from the Hebrew root קבל, that means "to receive." Kabbalah is usually understood to be "tradition," and the Kabbalah is understood to be a mystical tradition. Now our only problem is understanding the meaning of mystical. Mystical doesn't mean "magical." It isn't about getting God to perform tricks for us. It is about finding ways to get closer to God by getting ourselves closer to the best person we can be. It is about changing the world through changing ourselves. That is probably still confusing, so let's explain some more.

Kabbalah starts with the Torah. Tradition says that there are four levels to Torah study.

- **P'shat**: This is the literal meaning of the words. When one studies Torah on the *p'shat* level, one tries to figure out what every word means.

- **Remez**: *Remez* means "hints." It is the way we look in the Torah and learn about the "future history" of the Jewish people. On this level we see hints about the messiah, about the redemption, about the time when people finally perfect living together on the earth.

- **D'rash**: This level is one that works between the words. It is the place where midrash is made. The Torah first says that Abraham went on a journey and second says that he came to his destination three days later. *Drash* is trying to figure out what happened during those three days.

- **Sod**: This last level translates as "secret." It is the level where the Torah tells our story and gives us insights into how to grow into the best possible us.

When we study completely, when we study on all four levels, we get to פַּרְדֵּס *PaRDeiS*. This is the Hebrew word for "orchard." It is also a word for "paradise." When we get to the deep secrets of the Torah, the Kabbalah, we get back to the Garden of Eden, to a time and place where everything is perfect. Kabbalah is the path to make the world a place of prosperity, justice, truth, freedom, and maximum potential for all of humanity.

Rabbi David Aaron on Jewish Mysticism
(http://tiny.cc/iujc9)

Natan Starsky

My parents named me Natan after Rav Natan who was Rabbi Nahman's number one disciple. Just look at me. Black and white clothes. My *tallit katan*, my little tallit, hanging out. My *payot*, earlocks, hanging down.

<u>H</u>asid means "pious." My family lives a life where we try to get close to God through everything we do. My father is an artist (and I can't draw at all). We live in Tzfat so my father can be inspired by the place where Jewish mysticism grew and where he can sell his paintings to tourists.

I have four brothers and two sisters. My mother stays at home and takes care of us. Her *cholent* is my favorite thing she makes. She uses meat, potatoes, beans, onions, dried fruits and barley. She puts it in the stove before Shabbat begins and then lets it slow cook until Shabbat lunch.

School is my favorite thing to do in life. That, and sing and dance on Shabbat. I like studying Torah and Mishnah and our other Jewish subjects. I am also really good at math. I don't like writing essays.

When I grow up I am going to go into Yeshiva and study Talmud. I will not go into the army. Instead I will devote my life to study and getting close to God.

Lekha Dodi

Lekha Dodi was written by Rabbi Shlomo ha-Levy Alkabetz (1505–1584), a kabbalist from Tzfat. He arranged the poem so that the first letters of each stanza spell out his name.

After the מִנְחָה *Minhah* (afternoon) service, as the sun set over the distant hilltops, Rabbi Isaac Luria and his disciples would go out into the fields to stand on one of Tzfat's magnificent slopes. Gazing out at the view, they would open their hearts in song as the sun set:

לְכָה דוֹדִי לִקְרַאת כַּלָה פְּנֵי שַׁבָּת נְקַבְּלָה.

Lekha dodi, likrat kallah; P'nei Shabbat, n'kablah. This refrain concludes each of the nine verses of the song. There is hardly a phrase in the entire prayer that is not borrowed from somewhere in the Hebrew Bible.

The words of the chorus and the last two words of the hymn were taken from the Talmud. The Talmud relates that every Shabbat eve Rabbi Hanina would put on his finest garments and say, "Come, let us go out to meet the Shabbat Queen."

Rabbi Yannai likewise put on his festive clothes and declared, "Come, O Bride, Come, O Bride" (*Shabbat* 119a; *Bava Kama* 32b).

We no longer go outdoors to welcome the Shabbat Bride. But we do turn around to face westward in the direction of the setting sun that signals the arrival of Shabbat. This we do while reciting the last verse of *Lekha Dodi*.

The title *Lekha Dodi* is borrowed from Song of Songs 7.12: "Come, my beloved, let us go into the field, let us stay in the villages; let us go early to the vineyards..." Based on this verse, the kabbalist Rabbi Isaac Luria and his disciples used to go outside the city limits of Tzfat into the open fields to welcome the Shabbat with the psalms and hymns that are now the Kabbalat Shabbat service on Friday evenings.

The Ari

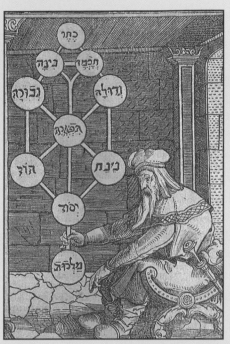

Rabbi Isaac Ben Solomon Luria was a sixteenth-century Kabbalist who revolutionized the study and practice of Kabbalah. He studied the *Zohar* and was responsible for adding a wealth of kabbalistic ideas. He left Spain to excape the Spanish Inquisition. Rabbi Luria developed the idea of צִמְצוּם *tzimzum*, God's exiling God's self from the region of the world in order to give space for the created world to be brought into existence. It is our job to work toward תִּקּוּן עוֹלָם *tikkun olam*, repair of the world. It is not a surprise that these scholars, who were in exile from Spain, figured out that God was in exile, too.

Rabbi Luria got his nickname the Ari (the lion) from the initials of *ha-eloki Rabbi Yitzhak*—the divine Rabbi Isaac.

1. What was the Ari's real name?

2. Why do you think the Ari spoke of God being in exile?

A Kabbalistic Text: God Goes into Exile

Here is a text. It retells the story of creation and adds some new understanding.

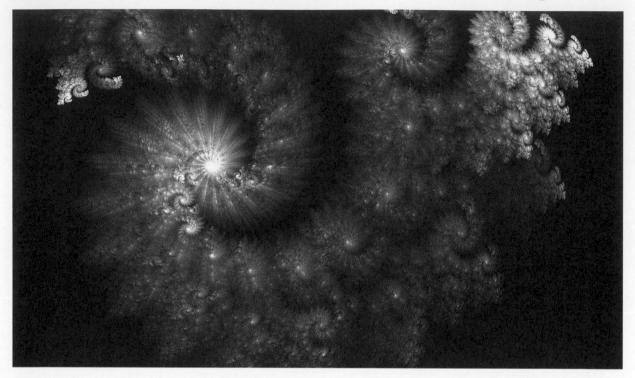

Before God created the world, God's light was everywhere. There was no empty space. Everything was filled with a light had no beginning or end. It is called the "Light with No End."

When God decided to create worlds, God had a contraction. God pulled back God's light from part of everywhere and left a space with no light. In that empty space God would create the world. In that space was darkness because none of the "Light with No End" was there. God was in exile from this space.

How did God create the world? God was like a person who took in a big breath, and then breathed out only a little bit, slowly. God breathed back only a little bit of light and the world was left almost completely in darkness. In that darkness God carved large boulders and cut huge stones to create a path to wisdom.

Retold from Howard Schwartz's *Tree of Souls*

1. Why *did* God need to create a space with no God?
2. Why *did* God need to put back a little of God's light?
3. According to this story how *do* we find God?

Tzfat, Sefardic City

In Tzfat there are two synagogues that are named for the Ari, Rabbi Isaac Luria.

The Sefardi Ari is the oldest of Tzfat's synagogues. It was once known as the Elijah the Prophet Synagogue. It was renamed for the Holy Ari in the sixteenth century. Tradition teaches that the Ari studied with Elijah in the small underground cave on the eastern side. Three holy arks are set into the thick southern wall with a colorful rose window above them.

The Ashkenazi Ari Synagogue was built after the Holy Ari's death. It was destroyed in an 1837 earthquake and rebuilt by the Italian philanthropist Yitzhak Guetta. In front stands a stone pillar with a fire pit for the old and sick on Lag Ba'Omer.

The real question is not why two Ari synagogues, but what are Sefardi and Ashkenazi?

In 586 B.C.E. Jews were exiled from the Land of Israel. They were taken to Babylonia. This was the Babylonian Exile. About seventy years later they were allowed to go back. Only some Jews returned to Israel; many stayed in Babylonia. Around the year 200 C.E. Romans drove most of the last of Jews left in the land of Israel out. Many joined the large mass of Jews that were still in Babylonia. However, because stories are never simple, there were now Jews in Egypt, France, Italy, and most of the other places that were part of the Roman

Ashkenazic *Haroset*

Ingredients

3 medium apples
½ cup chopped walnuts
1 teaspoon honey
½ teaspoon cinnamon
1½ tablespoons sugar
3 tablespoons red wine or
grape juice

Instructions

1. Peel, core and chop or grate the apples into moderately coarse pieces.
2. In a bowl, toss the apples with the walnuts, honey, cinnamon and sugar.
3. Stir in the 3 tablespoons wine. Keep in the refrigerator until it is served—at least six hours.

Sefardic *Haroset*

Ingredients

2 sweet apples, peeled
    and cut in small pieces
½ pound pitted dates
1 cup raisins
juice and zest of 1 orange
1 cup wine or grape juice
3 tablespoons sugar
2 ounces coarsely chopped walnuts

Instructions

1. Put the apples, dates, raisins, orange juice, orange zest and red wine into a saucepan and cook on very low heat, stirring occasionally, until the mixture is soft and mushy and the liquid is reduced.
2. Add the sugar.
3. Put the mixture in a bowl and mix together until well blended.
4. Pour into a serving bowl and sprinkle with the walnuts.
5. Refrigerate or serve warm.

Empire. Jews now went as far as China, but most wound up in Northern Africa, Western Europe, and Eastern Europe.

About 700 C.E. a new religion, Islam, got started and swept out of Iran, across Northern Africa, and into Spain. For a long time parts of Spain went back and forth between Catholic and Muslim rule. In 1492 the Catholics banished all non–Catholics from Spain. This resulted in many Jews moving to Tzfat. Sefardi is the Hebrew word for Spanish. Ashkenazi is the Hebrew word for German.

Here is the simple explanation of Sefardi and Askenazi. Jews who lived in countries ruled by Muslims became Sefardic and evolved one set of customs and traditions. Jews who lived in countries that were under Catholic rule became Ashkenazic and evolved another set of traditions and customs. Judaism split into two parallel but slightly different ethnic traditions of practice. Tzfat in the sixteenth century was essentially a Sefardic city, but a Sefardic city to which a number of Ashkenazim moved both for study and for commerce.

Ashkenazic Jews do הַגְבָּהָה *hagbah* (lifting the Torah) after the Torah reading; Sefardic Jews do it before the Torah reading. Many Sefardic Jews speak a kind of Judeo-Spanish called Ladino. Many Ashkenazic Jews speak a kind of Judeo-German called Yiddish. Sefardic Jews think that a תּ *Tav* and a ת *Tav* are both pronounced like a T. Ashkenazic pronunciation has a תּ *Tav* and a ת *Sav*, one pronounced like a T and the other like an S. Ashkenazic חֲרוֹסֶת *haroset* (the sweet stuff eaten on Passover) is often made out of apples, nuts, honey, cinnamon, and red wine.

One of many Sefardic *haroset* recipes uses figs, dates, sesame seeds, cinnamon, ginger, coriander, cayenne pepper, and red wine. These are only some of many such differences (and similarities).

Modern Israel is made up of both Sefardic Jews (47% of the population) and Ashkenazic Jews (53% of the population). There is some conflict, but also a sense that "we are all Israelis." The early Zionists were Ashkenazim, many from Russia and Eastern Europe. As soon as the State was established there was a huge influx of Sefardic *aliyah*. Ashkenazim still have a greater representation in the government and more economic success, but Sefardic Jews are gaining. Ethinic background is still an issue in Israel.

Synagogues to Visit

Yossi Bana'a (The White Tzaddik): This one is named for the third-century Talmudic sage whose tomb is supposed to be in the room next to the synagogue. A legend tells of the rabbi's son who got the fig tree in the courtyard to bear fruit out of season in order to pay his father's workers. The son was punished and did not live out the year.

Alsheich: Rabbi Moshe Alsheich lived and taught in Tzfat. This is one of the few buildings that survived the 1837 earthquake.

One of the Torah crowns in the synagogue dates from 1434.

Yosef Caro: This synagogue was built as a *Beit Midrash* (House of Study) and is said to have been the study hall of Rabbi Yosef Caro, 15th century, author of the *Shulhan Arukh*, one of the most important codes of Jewish law. The building was destroyed in the 1837 earthquake but was restored by Yitzhak Guetta.

Abuhav: Named for Rabbi Yitzhak Abuhav, a fifteenth-century Spanish rabbi. He designed this synagogue while still in Spain, and his disciples built it when they arrived in Israel. The dome is decorated with the symbols of the Tribes of Israel and musical instruments. There are three arks. The one on the right contains the Torah scroll traditionally reported to have been written by Rabbi Abuhav. It is taken out only three times a year.

Israel and You

אַרְצֵנוּ

This book is almost over. This is the last chapter. We could have included a lot more, but there is one more thing we have to do before we finish.

When you study mathematics, it is expected that there are things you will be able to do with numbers that are part of your life skills. When you study the Bible, the idea is that you will come to understand something about God and something about yourself. Bible books are supposed to make a difference. This has been a book about Israel. It is supposed to make a difference, too. It is supposed to help you grow your relationship with the State of Israel. But this book has not been enough. It has only been a beginning. The rest of the job is now yours. Like any friendship, it takes work to grow and keep it. You have to do things together. You have to learn about each other. You have to spend time together. This last chapter is about the things you can do with Israel.

Why Care about Israel?

Let's start with the obvious. You are Jewish, and Israel is the Jewish State. In the Talmud it says כָּל יִשְׂרָאֵל עֲרֵבִין זֶה בָּזֶה *Kol Yisrael aravin zeh b'zeh* (all Jews are connected). While we have a connection to every other Jew, not every single Jew is our friend. We want Israel to be your friend, not just because half of the world's Jews live there, not because the things in the Bible happened there, not because they speak Hebrew, not because Israel is the center of Jewish life and one major thing that all Jews have in common, not because Israel is the center and heart of Jewish culture, but because Israel is exciting and can change your life—the way a good friend does.

Here are some things you can do to keep Israel in your life.

A Map

Get yourself a map of Israel. It could be a large map that you keep on a bulletin board in your room or it could be a small map that you keep in the desk drawer. Every time you hear

a news story that mentions a place in Israel, find the place on your map. When someone mentions a place in Israel, find it on your map. When you are studying Bible or something else Jewish and the text mentions a place in Israel, find it on your map. If you are doing the big-map-on-the-bulletin-board thing, you may want to stick a pin in the place. This is a great way to grow your understanding of Israel by knowing where places are.

You can also do the opposite. Close your eyes. Point to a place on the map, then use your computer to find out about it. Here is the big idea: The more you know the map of Israel, the more comfortable you begin to feel with Israel. You are no longer as much of a stranger, and the places are not so foreign. It is not as good as visiting Israel, but it is a great start.

Find the following places on an Israeli map.

Here are some places we haven't talked about.

- Sderot_____
- Netanya_____
- Ramat Gan_____
- B'nai Brak_____
- Kiryat Shmoneh_____
- Kibbutz Yotvata_____
- Arad_____
- K'far Saba_____
- Ashkelon_____

Now use the Internet or an encyclopedia to find out one thing about each place.

Israel and the News

Israel is in the news just about every day. Israel is a continuing story. Sometimes it is about conflict with the Palestinians or Arab neighbors. Sometimes it is about steps toward peace. There are stories about medical advances, because Israel has some of the best medical research facilities in the world. Other times it has to do with electronics or even sports.

Here are three websites that connect to three Israeli newspapers. They are all good places to find out about Israel.

- http://www.haaretz.com
- http://www.jpost.com
- http://www.ynetnews.com

This is just the beginning of where you can find Israeli news. There are Jewish newspapers and magazines that have regular stories about Israel. There are Israel-oriented blogs and more. But most of all, there is conversation. When you find other people who want to talk about Israel, you will have connected with Israel and you will have begun to make a friend.

Israeli Music

Check it out: http://www.amichai.com/live. This website will take you directly to thirty Israeli radio stations—live! By jumping around the list you'll be able to find all kinds of Israeli music, ranging from rap to ethnic to folk to classical. Israel has a huge recording industry and is a major source of music. Some of it will sound really familiar. It will be just the kind of thing you listen to—except most of it is in Hebrew. Others artists will sound more European or African or Middle Eastern.

If you Google "Israeli Music" you will find all kinds of artists you can listen to and even download. Know that most of this music has nothing to do with anything religious, and most of it is Jewish only in the sense that it is created by Jews in a Jewish state going through the same kinds of experiences that you do. No matter what kind of music you like, you'll find some Israeli artists you'll like, too.

Israel Today

What is one news story involving Israel today? Find out!

_____

_____

_____

_____

_____

_____

_____

So What Would You Download?

Check out some Israeli artists and find one whose music you might like to download. Share the name and the web link.

_____

_____

_____

_____

_____

Israeli Dance

Immigrants to Israel in the 1920s were new to a life of collective farming. They expressed their desire to return to the land through dance. Israeli folk dance, with barefoot dancers in loose clothing leaping and running, reflects the life of a people returning to its own land.

While originally from Europe, Israeli folk dance has been influenced by the traditional dances of different ethnic groups in Israel. Many dances are choreographed to modern Israeli music, which is a blend of Western and Middle Eastern cultures.

Today Israeli folk dancing is done around the world in Israel, Europe, South America, the United States, Canada, Australia, and even Japan. Thousands of people participate in Israeli dance classes just for fun. In addition, folk dance troupes perform at festivals and events throughout the year.

Israeli Books

As much as Jews are The People of the Book, they are The People Who Make Books.

Today novelists like David Grossman, Alef Bet Yehoshua, and Amos Oz (to name a few) are world-class writers. There are lots more.

Then there is the Jerusalem International Book Fair (JIBF). Started in 1963, it is a unique biennial event that draws over 1,200 publishers from more than 40 countries who display more than 100,000 books in different languages.

The year 1995 marked the first time the fair had participants from the Arab world, including Morocco, Egypt, and Jordan, and they have continued to attend the JIBF. At the February 2005 JIBF, Palestinian, Arab, and Israeli writers participated in a unique literary enounter attended by numerous publishers, editors, and writers from around the world.

Israeli Things

Do you like shopping? Israel is a great place to shop—even when you are not there. Filling your house with Israeli items is a great way to build the connection.

Israeli Food

Israel is full of food, and Israelis love to eat. People come to Israel from all over the world. Israeli food has flavors from all over the world. When someone moves to a new place they bring their favorite foods with them.

Jews from the Middle East brought falafel, hummus, and te<u>h</u>ina with

Find one of the following on the Internet. Write down the URL.

Tzahal T-shirt _____

A piece of Israeli fashion _____

A mezuzah made in Israel_____

A painting by an Israeli artist _____

An Israeli *hanukkiyah* _____

An Israeli *kippah* _____

Israeli Recipes

Hummus

1 can of garbanzo beans
¼ cup tahina (sesame paste)
½ cup lemon juice
3 cloves garlic, finely chopped
1 teaspoon salt
1 teaspoon pepper
3 tablespoons extra-virgin olive oil

1. Pour all the ingredients into a big bowl.
2. Using your hands (or a potato masher) mush all the ingredients together until it feels kind of like peanut butter.
3. Use a spatula to put the hummus on a plate or in a small bowl. Drizzle some olive oil on top. (Israelis like to decorate their hummus with paprika or toasted pine nuts.)

Falafel Balls

Makes about 50 balls
1 cup of canned garbanzo beans
¼ cup chopped onion
1½ cups water
2 tablespoons chopped parsley
¾ cup soybean flour
10 chopped garlic cloves
2 teaspoons lemon juice
2 teaspoons cumin
1 egg
3 teaspoons paprika
1 slice of bread, broken up into crumbs
6 teaspoons baking powder
1 teaspoon salt
9 cups vegetable oil

1. Blend garlic, chopped onion, parsley, egg and garbanzo beans in a food processor.
2. Add soybean flour, lemon juice, cumin, paprika, bread crumbs, and baking powder. Blend some more.
3. Heat three cups vegetable oil in a wok or deep pan over medium heat.
4. Spoon out the mushy falafel mixture into your hands and roll into ½-inch balls.
5. Fry the balls in the hot oil until they're golden.

them. Falafel are fried balls of chick peas. Hummus is like Israeli peanut butter. Israelis put te<u>h</u>ina on sandwiches the way Americans put mayonnaise on sandwiches.

Jews from North Africa brought shakshuka to Israel. Shakshuka is a tomato stew that has eggs cooked on top. Jews from Asia brought Chinese food and sushi to Israel.

Jews from Eastern Europe brought kugel and latkes to Israel. Kugel is made from noodles. It is sort of like lasagna.

Jews from Western Europe brought schnitzel to Israel. Schnitzel is the name for chicken breast that has been breaded and fried. Israelis like to eat schnitzel with hummus and te<u>h</u>ina.

Jews from America brought pizza to Israel. Israelis like corn and tuna on pizza.

Israelis also make foods from things that grow in Israel. Israelis love salad. In Israel, salads almost always have cucumbers and tomatoes. Cucumbers and tomatoes grow all over Israel. Israelis eat salads at every meal.

Pomelos are like giant grapefruit, but they are sweet and juicy and easier to peel.

Israeli Movies

The first big Israeli film was a comedy called "Sala<u>h</u> Shebati". It starred Topol and was written by Ephraim Kishon. One of its most famous scenes was the forest namings. Topol, who plays a Yemenite worker, is planting JNF trees. A limo pulls up, and an area of the forest is donated to an American family who made a big donation. When the limo pulls away the JNF worker pulls down the sign and puts up a new sign naming the same forest for a new family. When another limo pulls up there is a new forest dedication, but Topol gets in the way, arguing that this forest belongs to the first family.

As with books and records, there is a prosperous Israeli film industry. Your neighborhood video store probably has some Israeli films in the foreign film section. If you check out the Internet you will find long lists of Israeli films, especially at imdb.com (Internet Movie Database).

Defend Israel

Almost wherever you go you can find somebody distorting the truth and turning Israel into a bad guy. One of your big jobs is to know enough to defend Israel. Israel is not perfect. You may not agree with everything Israel does, but Israel needs you to tell the truth.

You can't do this one if you don't follow the news. You need to know some history, too. But it is something you can learn

Film Festival

Many American and Canadian communities have Jewish or Israeli film festivals. Program your own Israeli film festival. Pick five movies to show.

_____

_____

_____

_____

_____

to do. Israel needs you to straighten out some of the lies that are told about her. It will take more study to get good at this, but you can do that.

Plan a Trip to Israel

Here is the last and most important thing you can do: go to Israel. It could be a bar/bat mitzvah celebration in Israel, a high school or college program, but you need to get there. You can go with your family or plan a year or half year of study there in high school, college, or beyond. You can go to Israel to volunteer on a kibbutz or an archaeological dig, or even to help the Israeli Army. But you need to go.

The best way to get there is to start planning (and maybe saving) now. Make it a topic of family conversation. Ultimately you can read and know a lot about Israel, you can care a lot about Israel, but until you go visit, the relationship between you and Israel will not be complete. We know that once you have been there, you will be planning how to get back.

So here is the bottom line: Get yourself to Israel. Don't just study about her, go and visit!

Joelle Jenkins went to Israel for six months during her junior year of high school.

Hey! It's finals week here in Israel. I am liking the finals schedule tremendously. It is the first time we are allowed to sleep to noon. Our finals start at 2 p.m. Thursday. We are heading off to the Negev. We will spend the weekend on Kibbutz Yahel, and then we begin our trek through the Negev to Eilat. One day we get to ride camels, and in Eilat we get to go snorkeling. I am not sure if I am excited or not for this trip, because I really don't want to walk in the desert.

As my trip in Israel comes to a close, I am thinking a lot about my whole experience here and how it has affected me. Before coming to Israel, many would ask why I chose Israel, and I was not really sure how to answer them. My whole life I have gone to temple, prayed for Israel, and said next year in Jerusalem as if it were routine. I am a Reform Jew, and I lived up to it. I would question prayers, not say ones I did not agree with, and I would question traditions.

I decided to go to Israel because it is the Jewish homeland, although I did not really feel a major connection to the country. I was an American. I believed what the news told us. I put some blame on Israel for the Israeli/Palestinian conflict, thinking that they could try harder and wondering why there was a lot of opposition to disengagement.

It was toward the middle of the trip that I began changing my mind. I felt myself becoming part of Israeli culture. When talking about Israel and the Israelis I began to say we, and when talking about the U.S. I caught myself saying "the U.S." and "Them", not including myself as part of them. I would see prayer books with English in them, and I was disgusted. I began learning more of the traditional prayers, no matter if I agreed with them or not. Israel was not just another country anymore; it was my homeland, and I could picture myself living my life here. Most of these changes of mindset for me were subconscious. I was not aware of these changes untill I looked back on them.

I am happy to be going home to see my friends and family, but it is going to be so hard for me. I am leaving a part of me here in Israel. I know I will be coming back. I cannot picture a life anymore without Israel, although I do miss Mexican food. I am considering moving to Israel for good. It is amazing here! Israel is the most self-critical nation I have ever seen. They form commissions after every military act performed, even if they won or there were barely any casualties. I no longer blame Israel for the Israeli/Palestinian conflict. They are trying.

"I will never forget thee, Israel. If I do, let my tongue stick to the roof of my mouth."

(Psalms 137.5–6)

I plan to go to Israel when_____

_____

_____.